Praise for

choose JOY

"I can't wait to meet [Sara] in heaven someday and thank her for her influence over my life...but until then I will do my best to follow this precious sister's lead of trusting Jesus no matter what, surrendering to His perfect plan, and choosing a life of unshakable, unending joy."   —Lindsay McCaul, recording artist

"CHOOSE JOY is a must-read book, full of love, hope, and grace, just like Sara. Her words, beautifully pieced together by Mary Carver, left me yearning to live with more intention. This book is a gift the world needs."

—Jessica N. Turner, author of *The Fringe Hours*

"CHOOSE JOY is a journey into joy from the most unlikely source—a woman who was well-acquainted with grief. Sara's story has lingered with me long after I closed the book, and I'm ever grateful to Mary Carver for writing it down."

—Emily P. Freeman, author of *Simply Tuesday*

"Sara was a rare soul. She did what most of us long to do: She found joy in the midst of heartache and loss...Through the gift of her words and Mary's pen, we can learn to choose joy, too."

—Kristen Welch, author of *Rhinestone Jesus* and founder of the *We are THAT family* blog

"Nodding in agreement, laughing, and pausing to consider life's bigger questions, this book reminds me of how much I do indeed have to be grateful. I am humbled to have entered into Sara's world through these collected writings and truly inspired to better choose joy in my own life's circumstances."

—Alexandra Kuykendall, author of
Loving My Actual Life and
The Artist's Daughter: A Memoir

"Your heart will be deeply stirred after reading this book, and you will be challenged to choose joy in all things despite your circumstances."

—Alli Worthington, author of *Breaking Busy* and
executive director of Propel Women

"Sara never stopped cheering me on to remember the joy set before me. She has entered the great cloud of witnesses, and when I least expect it, her words still hound me, and I remember how the race is worth it."   —Amber Haines, blogger

"In a world where so many are clamoring to be seen and heard, Sara encouraged us to live a simple life, putting aside self and asking how we can best serve God. Sara's message to choose joy in all circumstances, which she modeled so well, continues to influence those who read her words."   —Dawn Camp, blogger

"[CHOOSE JOY] serves as an incredible encouragement that even when life is not going the way we expect, choosing joy is always a wonderful option. The legacy of Sara's life lives on through the lessons in this book."

—Amy Allen Clark, founder of MomAdvice.com

"While pain lived in Sara, Sara lived in God. She chose to use that pain and suffering as a passageway, not a place to stay, and she ended up living a most remarkable, inspiring life. What a stunning legacy."   —Meg MacDonald, owner of M:M Music

"As I sat and read CHOOSE JOY, it seemed I could hear with the ears of my heart this young woman so full of life, this woman so full of dreams, this woman who learned and embraced every person, every moment as a gift to be cherished, tell me CHOOSE JOY . . . CHOOSE JOY."
                    —Sister Marie Hesed Champagne, SOLT

"This book tells the remarkable story of one woman's life, but it's really a message for all of us. Through Sara and Mary's words, CHOOSE JOY challenges readers to take another look at their lives and appreciate all the incredible blessings they have but might have taken for granted."
                    —Patrick O'Connell, director of NewThing

"You will feel the highs and lows of Sara's life as you read these pages. We don't control much of the direction our lives take us, but we absolutely choose how we will make the journey. So CHOOSE JOY!"
                    —Troy McMahon, lead pastor of Restore
                    Community Church

choose JOY

Finding Hope and Purpose When Life Hurts

SARA FRANKL
and
MARY CARVER

Faith
Words

NEW YORK BOSTON NASHVILLE

FaithWords
Hachette Book Group
1290 Avenue of the Americas
New York, NY 10104

faithwords.com

Printed in the United States of America

RRD-C

First Edition: January 2016

10 9 8 7 6 5 4 3 2 1

FaithWords is a division of Hachette Book Group, Inc.
The FaithWords name and logo are trademarks of Hachette Book Group, Inc.

The Hachette Speakers Bureau provides a wide range of authors for speaking events. To find out more, go to www.hachettespeakersbureau.com or call (866) 376-6591.

The publisher is not responsible for websites (or their content) that are not owned by the publisher.

Library of Congress Cataloging-in-Publication Data

Frankl, Sara.
   Choose joy : finding hope and purpose when life hurts / Sara Frankl and Mary Carver. — First [edition].
      pages cm
   ISBN 978-1-4555-6281-7 (hardcover) — ISBN 978-1-4789-6078-2 (audio download) — ISBN 978-1-4555-6279-4 (ebook)   1. Suffering—Religious aspects—Christianity.   2. Choice (Psychology)—Religious aspects—Christianity.   3. Joy—Religious aspects—Christianity.   4. Frankl, Sara.   I. Title.
   BV4909.F735 2015
   248.8'6—dc23
                        2015023596

To Mike and Jane Frankl, who taught by example that true joy comes from a relationship with Jesus.

Contents

Introduction   xi

1. Roses in December: On Dreams and Stories   1

2. Silver and Gold: On Losing Abilities   12

3. Here to Be Changed: On Facing Pain   28

4. Resting Quietly on the Heart of Jesus:
   On Dealing with Fear   42

5. Giving Up and Letting Go: On Expectations
   and Goals   57

6. Rainbows and Rain: On Wanting What You Have   71

7. Placed Purposefully: On Surrender and Trust   87

8. Everything Is a Miracle: On Gratitude
   and Praise   100

9. Giving What We Are: On Serving and
   Community   115

10. God's Best: On Being Thankful for What You Had   133

11. The Life You've Been Given: On How I Want to Be
    Remembered   147

12. God Is Awake: On Living and Dying Well   158

Acknowledgments   173

Appendix: Tributes to Sara   177

Introduction

Sara and I both began blogging in the spring of 2008, but our online paths didn't cross until the end of that year. Back then I went by a pseudonym (because the Internet was a scary place!) and she signed her blog posts with a childhood nickname. Over time, through comments and tweets and e-mail debates over the importance of watching *Friday Night Lights*, Gitz and Photoqueen became Sara and Mary. What really cemented our friendship, though, was a cookbook.

Sara's disease stole many things from her, including the ability to enjoy a lot of her favorite foods. But that didn't stop her from converting many a friend to the joys of frozen Oreos, proclaiming Almond Joy the worst candy bar ever and sugar-doused tomatoes the best garden treat ever—or enjoying a cooking blog. Sara loved reading Ree Drummond's blog, *The Pioneer Woman*, and followed along online when Ree and her husband traveled to India with Compassion International. When they returned, Ree wrote that her family would be sponsoring a few older children who were part of a Compassion program, and that she'd like to give her readers the opportunity to encourage and correspond with the children. Sara volunteered to partner with Ree and in April 2009 she announced that together they were sponsoring Tsegaye, a high school student in Ethiopia.

Later that year Ree published her first cookbook and made a stop in my city as part of her book tour. I bought a ticket for the book signing—and remembered Sara's connection to her.

When I met Ree, I asked her to sign a second cookbook for Sara. She knew exactly whom I was talking about, which—when I reported back to Sara—prompted her to say, "WHOA! Are you serious?!?! She doesn't know who I am, does she? Because I think that would make my brain explode."

Thankfully, Sara's brain did not, in fact, explode—but from there on out, our friendship was more than just conversation through casual blog comments. We shared prayer requests and TV references (a not-so-guilty pleasure for both of us), and I soaked up every hopeful, hilarious, joy-filled bit of Sara I could through the computer screen. See, at the time I was doing everything but choosing joy. I spent my days in a job I hated, missing my little girl, and I spent my nights alone missing my husband, who worked the late shift. I was looking for a new job and considering about half a dozen new careers while I was at it, and to top it all off, my husband and I were still feeling the sting of a failed church plant.

Joy was a foreign concept at that point in my life—and then I met Sara. I remember first reading her comments on other blogs, then finally clicking over to her site. As I dove deeper down the rabbit hole of online friendships and connections, I learned about Sara's disease. I learned that she was practically homebound and experienced major physical pain every day. This vibrant, funny, positive woman who had real reasons to be bitter or angry was encouraging others and cracking jokes and telling stories. She was choosing joy—and her circumstances were a whole lot harder than anything I was facing on my side of the screen. Reading Sara's blog and becoming friends with her was simultaneously inspiring and challenging, changing my heart and outlook on life more than I ever expected when I clicked on her name that first time.

Over the years I tried to love Sara well, driving hours to visit her in the next state over, loaning her my DVD copy of *Freaks and*

Geeks, helping friends organize a "spoil Sara schedule" that lasted for several months. But it paled next to the shining example of Jesus and joy she was to me. Sara loved me and prayed for me and taught me to step back, look at the bigger picture, thank God for the good things, and, for crying out loud, just laugh at the hard ones.

Two years after we began our blogs and entered the online community, Sara and I met in person for the first time. On a whim (and a last-minute vacation day request), I hopped in my car and drove north to visit Sara for the afternoon. It was a nine-hour round trip—and totally worth it. I was nervous; even though I'd given up my pseudonym by then and attended writing conferences where I met lots of bloggers, it was still a little weird to drive to a blog friend's house and knock on her door. As soon as I walked in and found myself in a tighter-than-expected hug, though, I knew I'd made the right choice. As Sara's friend Shannon says, "Sara hugged so tight, you never wanted to let her go. It was a hug that reached all the way inside."

We spent that afternoon laughing and crying, discussing dreams and families and books and jobs—and the adventures of Sydney Bristow in the TV show *Alias*. Though I drove to Sara's house planning to learn more about her, she insisted on asking me question after question—why didn't I like my job? What did I want to do instead? What was my dream? What was God calling me to do?

When I left, it was too soon (after all, we hadn't solved the mystery of my dream job or the last season of *Alias*), and I promised to make it back again. I did visit Sara one more time, and that time I brought along my three-year-old daughter. Sara loved kids, and even though she was mostly confined to her bed by then, she made my little girl feel comfortable, despite her fear of Sara's beloved dog, Riley, and an unfortunate incident in which my daughter locked everyone out of the bathroom…from the outside. She even sent us home with a new teddy bear that was promptly named Sara Bear.

After that visit my daughter prayed for Sara every day and slept with Sara Bear every night. And when I suggested we make a "Flat Sara" to take along on our everyday adventures? My daughter was all over it and determined to show Sara—through her flat self—a good time. When I sent Sara a picture of our first outing (to Red Robin, where Flat Sara was photographed next to a stack of onion rings), she replied, "That may be the cutest and sweetest photo I've ever seen in my life!!! I'm half cracking up and half almost in tears that you and your girl love me this much. I love it!" She also traveled with us to preschool, choir practice, and Disney World—and helped us make brownies and paper snowflakes. I think it tickled her to be a part of our lives that way, and it reminded us to be thankful for our many blessings and mindful of the joy in our everyday lives.

When Sara died, I found myself without words to describe what I felt. As a writer I'm not often speechless, but all I had then was stunned silence. Though I'd known toward the end that her death was coming, I couldn't comprehend that my friend was gone. My daughter accepted it more easily; that faith of a child truly is amazing to witness. She understood that Sara had been sick and in pain, and now she was safe and healthy in Heaven with Jesus—and for my daughter, that was that. For me it was harder to process that my friend, whose words I'd read daily for years though I got to see her "in real life" only a couple of times, would no longer be there, on the other side of my screen. Never before had I been more grateful for the long life of online journals—and I was even more grateful for the legacy that Sara had left all over my life and our corner of the Internet.

My daughter and I drove north one more time for Sara's funeral, this road trip much more somber than the one we'd taken months before. I answered as many questions as that pre-schooler could throw at me, though in truth I had more questions than answers myself. Today Sara Bear remains in a place of honor on my daughter's shelf, though most of her stuffed animals have been put away to make room for books and Barbies. And Sara will forever be a part of our family's story.

I loved Sara and treasured our friendship, but my life wasn't the only one she touched. Her friend Jessica shared, "Even though Sara was just in my life for a couple years, I'm a better person because of her, because she loved well. We shared so much—life's joys and trials, the ordinary and the extraordinary—and she was like family to me. Sara is the biggest gift blogging has brought me. Every time I sent her a photo of my kids, she responded with delight. And when my family visited her the joy she exuded as she played with my son and held my baby was breathtaking."

· Before she died Sara asked her friend Shannon to speak at her wake (instructing her not to cry because it would "make things less effective"). When the time came, Shannon painted a picture of her best friend with words—and few tears: "Sara did everything full throttle, both feet in, filled with intention and limitless enthusiasm, shown by the sparkle in her eyes for what most interested those she loved. She told me once that the most important gift you could give someone was your full and undivided attention. Sara knew that to live well meant to treasure moments and see them as gifts. She chose joy. Not happiness, which is as flimsy as a shirt blowing on a line in the breeze, but true heart joy, which sustains through obstacles, disease, death. She made the hard choices—every day...She lived—every single day." Sara's life—her positive outlook and trust in God, her determination to show her friends and family just how much she loved them, and her commitment to joy—has inspired countless blog posts, newspaper articles, sermons, discussion groups and Bible studies, and even tattoos. Giving new life to Sara's words and her message of hope with this book is one of the biggest honors of my life, a privilege second only to knowing her and calling her a friend. Walking back through her years spent in chronic pain and debilitating illness has been both heartbreaking and life-giving, as I've been reminded both of the crushing difficulty of her life and of the resilience of her spirit and determination to choose joy no matter what. This book will focus on her message of hope, gratitude, and joy despite circumstances, but understanding her background and circumstances is vital to fully appreciating Sara's story.

Sara's Story

Raised on a farm in northwest Iowa, Sara was the youngest in a tight-knit family of six children. A true child of the eighties, she dreamed of being Mary Lou Retton, Olivia Newton-John, and the Bionic Woman. She was a dancer who entertained her family by prancing around the house on her toes and a writer who spent hours in the yard writing short stories on her typewriter. Sara was active and social, involved in music, theater, and sports, as well as her church. Later she earned her bachelor's degree in English and communications, then went on to write for a trade magazine based in Iowa.

During her junior year of college, Sara was involved in a car accident that spurred the HLA-B27 gene, which is known to cause ankylosing spondylitis. Ankylosing spondylitis is an autoimmune disease, a form of arthritis that primarily affects the spine, although other joints can become involved. It causes inflammation of the spinal joints that can lead to severe chronic pain and discomfort. In the most advanced cases (like Sara's), this inflammation can lead to new bone formation on the spine, causing the spine to fuse in a fixed position.

Sara also had leukopenia, which means her white blood cell counts remained lower than normal and actually decreased when she was sick instead of increasing. This meant she had to be extremely careful around other people, because contact with someone with a slight cold could lead to her getting pneumonia.

Most pain medications didn't work to curb the disease or Sara's pain (some even caused reactions such as severe migraines, permanent damage to her digestive system, and anaphylaxis). To help her breathe and control her inflammation, she took steroids—which, unfortunately, caused her to develop Cushing's syndrome and experience extreme exhaustion, headaches, nausea, and rapid weight gain.

Finally, as Sara's body continued to attack itself, she developed an intolerance to a number of irritants found outdoors, as well as the air in her condo and many foods. These diseases and allergies stole Sara's ability to work and to drive, and eventually her ability to even leave her home. She passed away in 2011 at the age of thirty-eight.

Or, as Sara put it, in simple terms: "I have a disease. It sucks. When you have a cold, your body sends little Pac-Man cells to eat up all the bad germs so you can feel better again. My body gets confused and can't tell the difference between the bad germs and the rest of my body, so the Pac-Man cells just attack everything. And that ends up making me feel sick and in pain."

Given this overwhelming army of diseases that attacked her from the inside and out, Sara was a prime candidate for bitterness, self-pity, or depression. And who could have blamed her? But rather than dwell on her pain and her loss, Sara chose to trust in a God Who is good all the time and to be filled with gratitude, hope, and joy.

When asked how she defined joy, Sara said, "Joy is the

unwavering trust that God knows what He's doing and has blessed me with the opportunity to be a part of it—not despite what's happening in my life, but because of it. When everything earthly feels heavy, He gives me an internal lightness that can't be touched."

Sara didn't just choose joy for herself; she also shared it with and inspired it in her family, friends, and online community. More often than not, she ministered to that community by telling funny stories about her family that were so warm and vivid you could hear her smile through the screen; confessing embarrassing moments, childhood adventures, and current obsessions (which almost always included Oreos and *Alias*); and sharing her latest creations—doodles, canvases, buttons, and fonts—and challenging her friends to create something, too. It was simply impossible to know Sara without being moved—toward gratitude, toward creativity, toward hope and joy.

Sara chose to be joyful despite horrendous circumstances, pain that brings me to my knees just reading about it. But while nobody would have blamed her for shaking her fist, asking, "Why me?" or resenting the God she'd grown up worshiping, she chose a different path. I don't think it's possible to read Sara's words or hear her story without being changed. And I believe all of us who open our hearts to the message Sara has to share can look back at our own lives—difficult or challenging or unexpected as they may be—and say, as she did so often, "It's all good."

In 2008 Sara wrote, "My life is a difficult balancing act, but I am not being flippant when I tell you that I have a good life. I have a home, friends, love, and support. I have a cute dog, and I have the time to really be there for people when they need me. This is not the life I imagined for myself, but it's the life I've been blessed with and I won't take a moment of it for granted. And if you're taking a moment to read this, I'm not taking that for granted either."

choose
JOY

1

Roses in December

On Dreams and Stories

⚬—⚬—⚬—⚬—⚬—⚬

God gave us memory so that we might have roses in
December.
　　　　　　　　　　　　　　　　　—J. M. Barrie

*Before the accident and the disease, before the hospitals and the
steroids, before the blog and the walker and the pup, Sara Frankl was
a girl who loved life and lived it to its fullest. She loved writing and
leading worship at church, water-skiing and scrapbooking, spoiling
her nieces and nephews, and eating Chinese food. Blessed with an
abundance of gifts, Sara sang, danced, and acted throughout her
childhood. She played Anne Frank on stage during high school and
ran hurdles on the track team. And once upon a time, she dreamed of
being the next Mary Lou Retton.*

⚬—⚬—⚬

When I was young I really thought I was going to be a famous
gymnast. I now see the flaw in the plan as I didn't train or
take lessons or work out. But I'm telling you, I could go in our

backyard and do a roundoff like nobody's business. We lived on an acreage so I had a lot of wide-open spaces—and our yard was my own personal area to work on my floor routine.

I'd take the boom box (remember those?) out back, put on music, and dance, do tumbling runs, and always end with the dramatic flair of my arms in the air with my back arched...just like Mary Lou Retton. And somewhere deep down inside I just knew that some scout would be driving along that blacktop in the country, notice me, and whisk me away for Olympic training.

Then again, I used to think a talent scout would drive on that blacktop, hear me sing, and give me a record deal, too.

At least the pigs and horses were entertained.

Gymnastics wasn't Sara's only love. She used that big backyard for a dance floor, too—and kept dreaming of putting on her dance shoes even after she'd grown up and her body had stopped cooperating with her imagination.

I wanted to be a dancer so badly when I was little. A girl has to dream, and I knew how to dream big.

I think I would have been considered a contemporary dancer (if I actually had skill enough to know what I was doing), but I really wanted to learn ballet. I would walk around the house with my toes curled under, walking on the knuckles, in order to practice ballet like I was in pointe shoes.

Seriously.

And I'm not talking about a few steps. I would walk around. I would do leaps and jumps and land on the knuckles of my toes in an attempt to pretend I was *en pointe*. It looked so impossibly ridiculous that my family would have me do jumps and land like that when company was over. (So, apparently, if I couldn't be in ballet I would've been a shoo-in for a sideshow at the circus.)

. I have to admit, even though I can barely walk behind a walker these days, there is still something in me that can picture myself on stage. I was watching the season finale of *So You Think You Can Dance* tonight, and I realized that some crazy remnant of my childhood still exists deep inside of me that believes I can do what they can do.

Let me clear this up. I'm not delusional. I know I can't. But that part of me that knew how to dream big still knows how to imagine.

$$9 \quad 9 \quad 9$$

Much as she loved performing—every chance she got, according to her sister Laura—Sara also loved using her gifts to bless others and lead them to God. Even if that meant standing up in class and belting out "Amazing Grace" when her college professor requested it.

$$9 \quad 9 \quad 9$$

The recurring theme at my church was, "Don't just go to church. BE church." I often thought of that saying as I volunteered for different programs, but the phrase really came to life when random little moments to be church presented themselves on campus.

One class in particular, my African American literature course, presented a very unexpected (and uncomfortable) moment to share about my church. The professor apparently had attended my church on a Sunday when I had led worship and sung "Amazing Grace" a capella. I showed up to class on Monday and he started his lecture by talking to us about how spiritual songs were often started by slaves. He began talking about "Amazing Grace," and then told the class that I had sung it that weekend—and that he thought it would be a great idea for me to sing it, right then and there, for the class.

You can be sure I was horrified. First of all, I'd had no idea he was there when I sang, and second of all, the last thing I had intended to do in my eight a.m. class was open my mouth to sing. I wasn't even sure I had spoken to anyone yet that morning. So I made everyone shut their eyes so I could pretend I was anywhere other than the broken-down college building—and I sang. And a good number of the class showed up the next weekend to Mass. I have no idea if any of them continued going, but they had a reason to go that weekend, and that was something.

♪   ♪   ♪

Sara found herself in hot water like that more than once, but her can-do attitude and confident optimism (not to mention a healthy sense of humor) always seemed to triumph. This spirit led her to start a blog that eventually reached thousands of people around the world with a message of joy—but it started many years earlier.

♪   ♪   ♪

You know how people always say, "Practice makes perfect"? I think in my world the phrase is actually, "Habit makes able." I'm not one of those people who are always confident in what they do. It usually appears as though I am, but deep down I'm not.

I don't start out with or end with confidence in my abilities, but I always dive in headfirst assuming it will turn out fine. I'm weird. *I know.*

The habit that makes me able to do most things, I've discovered, is the habit of saying yes to people who need something— usually because I want to be helpful or make them happy. I will have absolutely NO IDEA how to do what they're asking, mind you, but I say yes anyway and dive in headfirst.

When we were in high school, I was staying overnight with my friends Katie and Sue Ann at Katie's house. At some point during the night Sue Ann had decided that she wanted to get her hair cut into a bob (they were all the rage back then). She had long hair that went halfway down her back, but Katie and I looked at each other and decided that it couldn't really be all that complicated. She held the pieces of hair and I used the scissors, and Sue Ann went home the next day with a whole new look. We weren't confident. Katie and I had momentary looks of *terror* on our faces that, thankfully, Sue Ann couldn't see. But she wanted it done, so we dove in headfirst.

(Thank heavens I got into the habit of cutting hair that way, because it's the only way mine gets cut now!)

Likewise, I didn't know I could design a Christmas photo card until a friend needed to find a cheaper way to send them out. I never imagined I'd be doodling for a living, until a few of you kept asking me to make them for you. When my friend Susie asked me if I could make a birthday invitation of Diego for her son I said sure, it would be easy. And then had the good sense to ask, "Who's Diego?"

I didn't do those things because I have a huge reserve of self-confidence. I did those things because I'm in the habit of saying yes. I am able to blog every day because I'm in the habit of it working. More than anything, I'm in the habit of believing if I just continue to step out in faith, that God will put what I need in front of me. That He'll line my path with the abilities and con-fidence that I'm lacking.

9 — 9 — 9

Even more than the physical gifts that allowed her to do the things she loved—even when they were things she'd never imagined doing, like cutting her friend's hair!—Sara appreciated the presence of her family and friends.

Susie was one of Sara's best friends, but she wasn't sure about Sara when they first met at college. "I was really quiet and extremely homesick, and I saw Sara and thought, 'Oh my gosh, why is she so happy?! Who is this girl? She needs to just settle down.' I'm not kidding. It was hard for me to see why anyone could be so happy." Luckily for both Sara and Susie, that wasn't the end of their story. One day, after Susie had an argument with her boyfriend, Sara insisted on taking her out to cheer her up. (As Sara said, "I quickly surmised that she was crying over a boy. Stupid boys. And lucky for Susie, we had a cure for crying. She'd be joining us for a drink and did not have right of refusal.")

Not only did the crazy evening out that followed cheer up Susie, but she ended up with a lifelong friend, a partner in crime, a sister of her heart. Susie said, "We couldn't believe we didn't know each other our whole lives. How did we not know each other our whole lives? I mean, she became my soul mate. She knew everything I was thinking, even when I didn't." The girls lived together during college in what they and their friends dubbed "the Big House," took road trips together, tried their hardest to get in trouble together (successfully when it came to getting caught with the giggles in church, but not so successfully when it came to overcoming their good natures with any real trouble), and celebrated their two-days-apart birthdays together.

As the years went on, their friendship just grew stronger as they walked together through the good times and the hard. When Sara heard that Susie's dad had died, for instance, she immediately went to help Susie's mom even though her own health was declining rapidly. And when Sara could no longer leave her home, Susie would visit often, bearing gifts of Sonic slushes (or a bottle of Moscato) and ready for a Brothers & Sisters marathon. Sara wrote about the way Susie and her other friends loved her well.

ɘ ─ ɘ ─ ɘ

They leave their busy lives and faster pace behind them at the door and settle into my slower-moving way of life. They don't rush me if I'm out of breath while I'm talking and they fill me in on conversations they all understand because they see each other while out and about, but that I miss while I'm here in my home. They show their love in the details, and they do it in an unassuming way that could easily go unnoticed. But I notice. Every little bit of it. And I am grateful.

I never cease to be amazed how, in every stage of my life, God has opened my heart to so many friendships. I love that I have friends who make me laugh until I cry. I love that some of my friends are so shy, until they get comfortable, and then they shock the life out of me with things they say or do. I love that some friends are intellectual and planners. I love that other friends go totally on emotion and spontaneity abounds. I have friends who are so much like me I think we may be the same person, and I have friends who are so opposite of me they keep me looking at life from different angles. I love that God knew I needed all of it and placed me right where I needed to be to find each and every one of them.

A number of people in my life are soul mate kind of friends. These are the people that I can maybe remember the first time I met them, but have no idea how we got from saying hello to knowing each other backward and forward because getting to that point usually took only one conversation. These friends are all such an essential part of my day-to-day life. They are the ones who so effortlessly let me live vicariously through them and their families, making my life feel absolutely whole and complete. I've not only been welcomed into their families but their extended families as well. I get to be a part of their kids' lives, but more importantly they don't mind that I love their kids like my own. They put up with the crazy dog and come hang out at my place

with me anyway, and the ones who live far away keep in touch
like we live just down the block.

I am blessed, people.

✦ ✦ ✦

Before she'd ever heard of ankylosing spondylitis, Sara treasured every
moment she had. She lived life to the fullest, enjoying her career, her
hobbies, and—more importantly—her family and friends. So when
she began losing these abilities and gifts she found she didn't have
regrets. Instead she was thankful for the opportunity to have lived
a beautiful life—and for the chance to continue choosing to live a
beautiful life, even if it wasn't the one she'd hoped for or planned.

✦ ✦ ✦

I used to work at a magazine in town, which has long since
been bought out and moved to California. I'm pretty sure the
name isn't even the same anymore. I look back now and realize I was so incredibly lucky to get a little piece of my dream
before this disease took away my freedom to work. I got to be a
part of getting a magazine published. I was able to write articles
and have my name in print. I got to travel to trade shows in
Chicago and Denver, and did interviews with major companies.
I got to be a part of something that is tangible and that's pretty
amazing to me.

I think a lot of my life, looking back, worked out that way. I
was never a major player at a magazine, but I got to be a part of
producing one. I was never a well-known singer, but I was appreciated in my community. I only sang at church and weddings and
funerals, but I think I touched people when I sang and I know
they offered me a lot when they listened. I was never a celebrated
actress but I got to be in plays and musicals and relished every
moment.

It's amazing that when you look at what you have, instead of what you won't or don't have, you usually see that in one form or another you've gotten what you wished for. It may not have been yours for long enough, or it may not have been as big as you dreamed it would be, but it was there.

That's why I really think I started my blog. I got tired of telling people what I used to do and who I used to be. I used to be a writer. I used to be a singer. I used to love to dance. When my friend's daughter Alex was a little girl we would spend a lot of time snuggling on the couch and talking about what she dreamed of doing or being. One day she looked at me and said, "When I get bigger I'm going to be just like you." Then she cocked her head and looked right in my eyes, obviously wondering what exactly that meant. Her eyes lit up and she declared, "I'm going to be sick!"

After I picked her mom up off the floor and revived her from her faint, I did my best not to bust out laughing and explained to her that I liked doing a lot of things, and she should just be whatever made her happy. But for the record, Alex, I'm a writer.

9 — 9 — 9

Sara was more than a writer, though that was how so many of her friends first got to know her. She was a singer, a dancer, an actor, and a runner. She was a photographer, a scrapbooker, a dog lover, and an aunt extraordinaire. She was a volunteer, an editor, a dreamer, and an encourager. She loved losing herself in a good story—whether that meant a marathon viewing of her favorite TV show or listening intently to a friend share her challenges and joys. And she was an inspiration and a teacher, a living example to her friends and family of choosing joy and hope through the most painful of circumstances.

9 — 9 — 9

"If you want the rainbow, you gotta put up with the rain."

Yep, I'm quoting Dolly Parton. I love that quote so much you'll probably hear me say it more than once, because that little sentence pretty much sums up my day-to-day life. In my body there is a constant rainstorm raging—a storm of debilitating disease, pain, limitation, and progression. At thirty-five years of age I have found myself homebound and having to give up every freedom and ability I used to treasure and enjoy. I can count on my hands the number of times I stepped foot outside of my house in the past year, and all but one of those times were for doctor appointments. There isn't one function that my body can perform without medication and my ability to do something as simple as type this post changes on a dime.

I have no career, no husband and kids, no financial security, and no potential to change any of those things.

And I've never been more at peace in my entire life.

I've discovered that when everything is taken away, when nothing is left but the core of who you are, that's when you have to make a choice. I can either hide inside and let the fear of getting struck by lightning paralyze me, or I can stand out in the rain to be washed free of everything but the comfort of a God Who would never let me fall. I choose every day to be washed free.

It's not easy, but it is simple. I put up with so much rain every day, but the rainbows I am given are fantastic. I have food, shelter, clothing. I have friends who love me, not despite all of my limitations, but with them. I write every day on my blog—and people show up! This blog has been a connection to the outside world that I didn't realize was missing until it fell into my lap. I have an obnoxiously cute, spoiled, and ornery pup who keeps me company 24/7 and brings joy to my otherwise quiet days.

I am so blessed, people.

But the reason I am happy is that I choose to look at my blessings more than my burdens.

The burdens are persistent; the pain is relentless. I walk with crutches and it takes me longer to get up out of a chair than it takes my friends to get up and walk the length of my condo and back. But I know that if God didn't have a purpose for my illness He would have taken it away from me by now. So I take it humbly and pray that if He has a purpose for me, I am paying attention so I don't miss the opportunity to serve. I'm okay with not knowing why this is happening to me because I know He knows why.

It's not about me; it's about what He can do with me. My job is simply to pay attention and enjoy the rainbows.

2

Silver and Gold
On Losing Abilities

Too many people miss the silver lining because they're expecting gold.
                                        —Maurice Setter

Blessed with many physical abilities and an outgoing personality, Sara was active—in her church and community, with her friends and family, at work and at play—until she simply could not ignore her body's refusal to play nice. From losing the lung capacity to sing or the energy for nights out with friends to realizing she needed a walker to move from room to room in her condo, the place she could no longer leave as she added homebound *to her résumé, Sara's abilities were stripped away one by one.*

Sara didn't sugarcoat the pain of these losses—but she didn't dwell on it, either. Here, in her own words, she shares the breadth of emotions she experienced as she said goodbye to abilities and futures and stages of life.

When I stopped dreaming I could run, I knew for sure my life had changed permanently.

Over the course of the last fourteen years, my disease and my life have changed dramatically. I won't go into a play-by-play for you, partially not to bore you to tears and partially because all of the years tend to run together after a while.

Once the diagnosis of ankylosing spondylitis was put on the table, though, everything about my body started making sense, and things that I didn't know went together turned out to be symptoms of the disease. The pain, the digestion problems, the night sweats, the bouts of iritis. Ahh, the good old days.

Things have gotten more complicated since then with breathing issues, swelling of joints, and exhaustion. I also have leukopenia, which basically means my white counts remain lower than normal, and actually decrease when I'm sick instead of increasing. This means I have to be ridiculously careful about being around someone with the sniffles for fear of getting pneumonia, which has become somewhat of an expected yearly ritual for me.

Living in the now is the easiest way to handle my life. It all changed when I realized that in my dreams at night, I was walking with a cane or crutches. And in my waking thoughts I can't imagine I ever ran track or jumped over a hurdle without it being painful. I don't remember what it felt like to not have pain, and while that was upsetting at first, I think it is actually easier this way. I don't long as much for something I can't imagine. I think if I dreamed I was running every night, waking up to the reality of having to figure out how to get out of bed would be crushing.

It's hard for people to understand that just because I'm not complaining, it doesn't mean I'm getting better. It's just that when you ask me how I am, I'm more likely to tell you how I am despite my disease, not because of it. I am more than that. I'm more than a sick person.

I'm a person who is sick—and as I often tell my mother, my body is brutal but I'm okay.

ꝯ ꝯ ꝯ

As Sara's disease progressed, her body constantly found new ways to stymie her efforts at a normal life. Forced to constantly reevaluate her abilities and determine what was possible on any given day, Sara still focused on the positive even while acknowledging her losses.

ꝯ ꝯ ꝯ

I write a lot about the silver lining. That's not just some sort of "Pollyanna-ish" way to look at life for me. I have a quote on my wall by Maurice Setter that says, "Too many people miss the silver lining because they're expecting gold." I love that quote not because of the optimistic silver lining, but because of its focus on the expectation of something better.

I think our expectations of what we want life to be often overshadow the good things that are already in front of us—and that's when we miss the silver lining. All God asks of us is to live the best life we can with what we are given. In other words, we are all given different blessings and different crosses to bear, which means we can only take care of what's in front of us in that moment and do the best we can.

As my life changed over the years, these truths proved to be something I needed to hear. I needed to remind myself that my old gifts were gone, and they didn't serve me in living my best life anymore. I had new gifts and crosses given to me, and I had to rethink how to live my life with them. It took a while to find my new normal, and that continues to change daily. But when my focus is on living the best life I can with what I have in that moment, I always find my silver lining. I'm not expecting the gold I *used* to have. I'm not looking for the gold that I think I *should* have. I'm looking at the silver right in front of me and saying thank you every day.

This applies to my body and my health, too. I am always prefacing any plans I make with the stipulation that I won't know until the day of if any of it will happen.

Back when I was able to get out and about, my friend Meg picked me up one night to go watch our friend Susie's husband play in his band. I knew before we left that my day hadn't gone smoothly, but I was sure I could push through the pain and go with them. During the very short ride to Main Street, the shooting pains in my leg had me shifting around trying to find a comfortable way to sit. We got to the bar, I got out of the car and took about three steps on my crutches—and I was stuck. I couldn't stand up straight, couldn't walk to the bar, couldn't walk back to the car. (Yes, it was as embarrassing as you are imagining.) Susie and her brother helped me to the car, and Meg drove me straight back home.

I was hoping for gold, but I wasn't expecting it. Deep down I knew there was a huge chance the night wasn't going to play out as I had hoped—but I didn't miss the silver linings. My friends were there to help me, and Meg wasn't worried about missing the first set. Instead, she made sure I got home okay. And here's the biggest silver lining of them all: all of those people would try again with me anytime. Really, how can I be anything less than grateful for that?

Now, let me just say that sometimes disappointment weighs heavy on me. But in my disappointment, the same rules still apply: I do the best I can with what I have. Is it usually all I want to do? No. But in the end, focusing on the silver lining is what gets me through the day.

I really think, in this life, we find what we are meant to do when we stop focusing on what we are kept from doing. I have to remind myself sometimes, but the more I acknowledge that silver lining, the less I notice the gold that's out of reach.

𝄢 — 𝄢 — 𝄢

Going out with friends and ending up back at home was disappointing for a social person like Sara, but other losses were bigger and more devastating. The ability to drive was a big one, and here she looks back on the day she realized she no longer needed a driver's license. In her typical fashion Sara shares her story with humor and honesty and ends up working her way to joy despite the pain.

𝄢 — 𝄢 — 𝄢

It was almost a month to the day after we celebrated my birthday when my friend Susie called. She was telling me about some event that had happened while she was getting her license renewed, and my heart almost got stuck in my throat. Since I hadn't driven anywhere in ages, it hadn't even occurred to me to check my license—and sure enough, it was expiring the very next day.

Susie and I both panicked, but she was out running errands with her boys and said they would pick me up and take me to get it renewed. I bustled around as fast as I could to change and get presentable for the photo, my main concern being the fact that five years ago I took a really good driver's license photo, and now I had been on steroids and looked like Theodore, the fullest-cheeked chipmunk of the bunch.

So when Susie picked me up in the sweltering Iowa heat, and I had on a sleeveless turtleneck, I thought she was going to drive right into the building because she was laughing so hard at me. My theory that the turtleneck helped cover up some of the steroid look of my neck only made her laugh harder. And through the insanity of all of this, reality still hadn't hit me.

My friend was picking me up to get my driver's license renewed because I could barely walk to her car on crutches, let alone drive. My biggest concerns were what my photo was going to look like and that I didn't want to retake a written test that I'd barely studied for when I was sixteen, for fear I wouldn't pass. Can you say *denial*?

It wasn't until we were pulling into the parking lot that it dawned on me. It wasn't until that moment that I looked at Susie and said, "You know...I couldn't pass a driving test. They'd watch me try to get into the driver's side of the car and tell me no before I ever turned the key."

Her eyes got sad and she said, "I was wondering if you were going to mention that."

I can still feel the knot in my stomach that I got with the realization that I was like my Grandpa Joe when he had Alzheimer's and they had to hide the keys to his truck because he wouldn't hand them over. He didn't want to let go of that part of his life, and couldn't accept the fact that it wasn't safe.

But I kept thinking...what if? What if they come out with a new medication and I suddenly do better and then I could drive and it would be harder to convince them to give me a license? What if the summer was better than the spring that was supposed to be better than the winter that I had hoped would be better than the fall? *What if?*

This is the only excuse I have for entering the Department of Transportation, trying to act like it was totally normal to walk in on crutches, and getting my license renewed. It's the only excuse I can give for answering all of the worker's questions honestly— until he kept asking me about my disease. Asking me if I ever jerk in pain, if it would be a problem when driving, if it was something I was concerned about. And I stood there, sweating in my turtleneck because I was trying so hard not to jerk in pain from the nerve zing that was pulsing in my leg—and I told him the only truth I could, that my doctors hadn't put any restrictions on me and they knew all about my condition.

I didn't mention the fact that we had never discussed if driving was a good idea or not.

To put your minds at ease, I didn't so much as open a window to my condo over the last eight months, let alone go for a joyride. My car has sat in my garage with a dead battery for almost a year now. Driving was something that I hadn't been able to do for a long time, but it wasn't until I stood there—feeling the burning realization—that I knew I had yet one more thing in my life I had to let go of.

I love this phrase: "Blessed is the person who finds out which way God is moving, and then gets moving in the same direction." It took me months to finally make the decision to let go of the thing that kept me from moving in the direction my life was already headed.

My nephew Thomas is turning sixteen this summer, and since he needs to get a car and I need to get rid of one, it was a pretty good match. And it turns out that the minute I let go of the notion that I needed life to change, rather than to change my life, the knot in my stomach went away. The moment I stopped trying so desperately to walk against the tide in which my life was flowing, I was relieved.

෧ ෧ ෧

Though she learned to accept her limitations and to choose joy and gratitude as her disease progressed, Sara wasn't always so accepting. She shared an essay on her blog that she'd written in 1997, before her diagnosis, when she was facing incredible pain while also finishing her college classes and working part-time at an advertising agency.

She wrote in her blog, "Most of the time back then I was able to grit my teeth and deal with the emotional roller coaster I was on, trying

to map out what my new future was going to look like. I knew how I
was supposed to be handling it, but the stability or acceptance I feel
today was still a long way away back then. It was hard for me to read
this, but I'm going to share it with you so you don't think I got sick and
immediately jumped to acceptance with this.

"There were moments when my spirit hurt so much more than my
body, and the night I wrote about back then was the worst of them.
The following is my low point, back in 1997, and reading it makes me
wish I could go back and tell that girl that her health would get worse,
but her spirit would be fine."

9 — 9 — 9

"Sing to the Lord with shouts..." But the "of joy" part was
never really heard. I watched. I listened. And I felt such an ache
inside of my heart I thought it might stop right there and then. I
think it's what people call despair. That feeling of being so alone
when there are so many people near you that you wonder if you
will ever experience joy again.

It all seemed like the cruelest joke anyone could play. I was
listening as the guitars and piano thundered together as though
they were connected. And a feeling of exuberance and anticipa-
tion consumed the chapel with the filling breath, turned in a
moment to a song. Their voices sang. Friends turned around to
say hello to each other and everyone in the chapel was a community. A community of support, of understanding, of believers.
What should have been an inspirational scene, I am ashamed to
say, left me alone and panic-stricken.

Alone. I was there with all of them, yet very separate. It was
as if I was watching on a big-screen TV, big enough to be true
to life. But I was in my easy chair watching it happen to other
people. I was alone in the lobby seeing, but not feeling, that connection, that wonderful sense of celebrating Christ with one

another. As they sang with shouts I cried with tears and I cried alone. I couldn't breathe and all I could hear over and over in my mind was, "Sing to the Lord with shouts..."

Shouts. I wanted to shout. I even wanted to shout to the Lord. The part that scared me was what I wanted to say. I had worked for so long at accepting and trusting that what has happened to me will work out. That it will have its purpose and somewhere I am growing and learning to be a better person. But in that moment I simply wanted to know why. Trust? Have a deeper faith? Why me, why now, and why in this way? I had just watched more than eighty people taking part in something that used to be my life. I watched them in those split seconds feel that connectedness that reminds us continuously of why we are all on this earth—to be witnesses to one another.

Witnessing. I guess that's the one thing I've tried to do with my pain. I tried to be the best little invalid that I could be. But as I sat there crying so hard I couldn't breathe and praying with all my might and sincerity to please, please have my life back, I wondered where all of this had really taken me. I prayed so hard for the feeling in the pit of my stomach to go away. I begged to feel nothing rather than feel this. I felt as though I was grieving for something somewhere. But I didn't know what it was. Just something. Just who I used to be. Just how I used to feel. And even though I prayed with my entire being, the feeling was still there. I knew I had to get ahold of myself. I had to get away.

Away. But where could I go? I thought of my apartment but it was too much of a reality. I needed a cabin in the woods where no one could find me. Where I could go until this feeling was gone and my acceptance was back. I didn't want to see anyone who knew me. I didn't want to see pain in anyone's eyes when they saw my pain. It's like a mirror reflection that is sometimes comforting because I know they care and sometimes terrifying when it becomes reality that this is happening to *me*, and that I cause this pain for others. In time I calmed down enough to reason with myself. I had just panicked. It would be better later.

Panic. I guess that pretty much sums it up. I can go along and do my best to do what's right, but in the end there is always that panic that reminds me of what I had and what I want back. It stares me in the face on that big-screen TV that's big enough to be true to life. And I can't run from it. So what's left? I can pray.

Pray. Pray for more faith. Pray for more trust. Pray for forgiveness in this self-absorbed weakness when I should learn to be grateful instead of beating myself up for being less than what I was. Pray that somewhere in this I stop grieving for that something somewhere. Pray that I can be faithful to the struggle and become whatever He chooses for me. Pray that in the end, when I look back on this struggle, I will be grateful I had the chance to panic—because hopefully, it will help me discover peace.

❧ — ❧ — ❧

In time Sara did discover peace and generously spread that peace and the joy she chose with others, even when they asked the hard questions, such as, "If God knew you would get this disease, why did He give you talents that you would eventually lose? Why not give you talents that could be used throughout your life, with or without this disease?" Sara graciously answered this question on her blog, revealing wisdom and gratitude that ran so much deeper than legs that could dance or vocal cords that could sing.

❧ — ❧ — ❧

I have to separate the gifts that were given to my body by genetics, from the gifts that were given to my spirit by God. We are given our bodies from our parents. Those genetics provide us all with the same basic body structures, but different parts of those bodies excel in different people.

Maybe your lung power and your leg muscles have made you a powerful long-distance runner. (I didn't get those genes.) I was given a set of lungs and some vocal cords and an ability to hear rhythms and notes, which just happened to work together to produce somewhat decent singing. All of that is physical, a genetic talent, but if you add to it the gift of my spirit, the result is the ability to feel and communicate the meaning of the words in order to bring a level of emotion and feeling to a song.

My vocal cords, strictly speaking, are a genetic gift. It's when I add my own spirit to the song that it begins to make the singing an "experience"—something that reaches people on a deeper, more emotional or more spiritual level. Do you see the difference? Most of the talent is genetic, but the gifts we bring to the talent to make it fulfilling are spiritual.

I had a lot of genetic talents this disease has stripped from me. I used to love to sing, I used to love to dance. I craved being able to work out and exercise. I also used to love to water-ski at the lake, and turn cartwheels and do roundoffs with the little kids. I used to perform on stage in high school and community theater. I was a cheerleader and ran track, running hurdles and doing the long jump. I had a wide array of interests and was certainly never bored.

I can't do any of those things anymore, those things I used to be able to do because of genetics. Without my physical body working correctly, they became impossible. But it's the gifts of my spirit, given to me by God, that were there along with my body—and those gifts remain after the disease has made my body, in many ways, useless.

While I loved to sing, what I really loved was the emotion that went into it and the connections I felt with the people I sang for. While my physical voice helped that along, the real part of that was spiritual and emotional. Those gifts from God remain and I have those moments of connection with family and friends still.

While I enjoyed exercise and physical activities, part of that was a way to burn off stress or deal with things going on in my life. I remember a moment when I was in college. As I walked down the basement steps, I jerked in pain, couldn't catch myself, and fell down the stairs. I was in pain, but I was even more frustrated because not only was I losing abilities, I was losing physical ways to cope. I wanted to hit something or go running or even obsessively clean to keep busy, but I couldn't do anything. My physical body failed me, but God never took away the gifts of my spirit.

I still had the desire to think analytically and write my thoughts so I could learn how to deal with them. I still had the desire to be positive and find the good amidst the bad. I still had the desire to learn better ways of coping, and He provided me with patience and fortitude and understanding and compassion and empathy.

This disease has taken away some talents that genetics gave me, but God never has. This disease has taken things from me, but it can't take away the spirit that God put inside of me, the core of who I am as long as I choose to nurture that side of myself. And like everything in life, because of free will, it's my choice. One I'm grateful I get to make.

$$\mathcal{9} \quad \mathcal{9} \quad \mathcal{9}$$

In the summer of 2009, Sara left her home for the last time. Her parents took her to a doctor's appointment and they quickly realized that exposure to the outdoors was more than her body could bear. The following weeks would prove this true with immense pain and difficulty

*breathing, and Sara faced the reality that she would not be able to
leave her home again.*

9 — 9 — 9

The direction my life is heading is simply not pretty. And talking about what that means for me, if I look at life realistically, means a lot of loss. For me to process that, I have to give myself a chance to sit for a moment and look at that reality. To acknowledge it, to mourn it, to let it go. That's hard for people to listen to because their first instinct is to tell me I shouldn't look at the future, I can't give up hope, I can't let myself go there. But I *have* to go there. It exists and pretending it doesn't isn't going to make it go away.

Trust me when I tell you I have hope. If some miracle happens to me tomorrow I am going to embrace it with every fiber of my being. But I also have to equally embrace the not-so-fun stuff. If this is my life, if this is where I am, then this is where God is, too. And if I'm wasting all my time and energy trying to pretend the future doesn't look like it does, then I'm wasting God's time as well. I know that I need to face what life is looking like now so I can accept it, hand it to Him, and find joy in the midst of it. It would be nice to go around it, but the only way is through it.

I think because I have been so diligent about isolating myself and keeping things consistent for my body and health, it just wasn't clear to me that I was still getting worse despite the lack of exposure. Before I went to my doctor's appointment, there was still some piece of me that thought my body's reaction to the outdoors would just be a hurdle. I was still thinking of masks and oxygen and ways to get around this, but there is no way around this.

I am completely and totally, from here on out, confined to my home.

No open doors or windows, no sitting on the patio or letting Riley go for a walk. No friends' homes, no movies, no church, no outings. I won't ever again sit by a bonfire to watch a sunset. I won't smell the fresh dew on the grass in the early mornings when the air is crisp and the lake is smooth as glass. No weddings or funerals or graduations or school plays. More than all of those things put together, I think of my nieces and nephews—the lives they have ahead of them—and my heart aches as I become a supporting player watching from a distance.

But it is what it is.

What I'm going through now, because I left my home for a few hours, is something my body just can't do again. I was expecting the level of pain from the extra movement and short ride in the car, but the issue with my lungs and entire body reacting to everything and anything they were exposed to was far more than I imagined. And the problems with the resulting medications have simply added to the intensity of it all.

So, life has difficult times. That still doesn't mean they are *bad* times; it just means we have to deal with what is in front of us when it's in front of us. For now, I'm adapting to this challenge. I'm taking my moments that require rest, taking my moments that require me to challenge myself and push, taking my moments of sorting through the realities and taking my moments of joy in the middle of it all. I really am dealing with this okay and my goal in life hasn't changed: I'm simply going to fulfill God's plan by living the best life I can with what I am given.

9 — 9 — 9

Sara knew that day outside her condo might be her last one—and she intentionally savored each moment of fresh air and freedom (and French fries). It would be easy to read her words about that day and question whether she'd have been so positive and thankful had she known just how bad her pain would become as a result of the trip. But everyone who knew Sara can answer that question with a resounding YES. Never one to dwell on what might have been or say, "If I'd only known," Sara lived in the present, choosing to smile when the sun shone—and when it didn't. And if she looked back on this day, she was surely glad to have enjoyed every bit of it.

ѹ ѹ ѹ

With my doctor, Annie, we talked through my prognosis, my medications, my options for what I could take to help with my lungs and the accompanying symptoms. We talked about some heavy topics and laughed about dumb jokes. She hugged me three times and we both knew that after fifteen years of being her patient, I wouldn't be coming in to see her again. She would make my medical decisions, but it would be through home nursing now so I won't have to make an extra trip out of my house again.

As Mom and I walked into the parking lot and Dad pulled up with the car, I stood outside the door and decided I wasn't getting in until the sun peeked out from behind the clouds. Mom and I talked about the perfect temperature and refreshing breeze. We talked for a moment about the things we'd discussed in Annie's office, and I told her that no matter how life progressed for me from that point out, it was okay. I was good with it, God and I were good with it.

Then the sun came out.

And Mom said she thought God was good with me, too.

My body isn't doing very well now. I'm in pain. I'm not breathing well, my eyes and ears and throat burn. The steroids and breathing treatments bring their own host of issues that leave me feeling unwell. I'm very tired.

But all I can think about is how blessed I am that Annie has taken care of me all these years, treated me with respect and love, and will continue to have my best interest at heart, even from a distance.

I can close my eyes and feel the breeze, feel the sun on my face and see the bright orange color that rests on the inside of my eyelids when they are closed and facing the sunshine. I can smile remembering that, for a few fleeting minutes, Mom, Dad, and I sat in those patio chairs I'd been longing to relax in and ate McDonald's French fries just because we could. After all, the damage was done and we were determined to take our moments.

A lot of things aren't going right because I left the house on Thursday. But I choose the joy. I choose the conversation, the relationships, the breeze and the sunshine.

And I especially choose the French fries.

I choose the joy. When something is going badly and I'm dwelling on it, I think instead of something for which I am grateful. I swear to you, it's as simple as that. You just have to decide today, and again tomorrow. And before you know it, you'll have an attitude of joy more than any other attitude you have at your disposal.

3

Here to Be Changed

On Facing Pain

❧ ❧ ❧ ❧ ❧ ❧

We are not put on earth merely to satisfy our desires,
to pursue life, liberty, and happiness.

We are here to be changed, to be made more like God
in order to prepare us for a lifetime with him.

—Philip Yancey

*Because of Sara's disease and her body's resistance to medication, she
was in incredible pain at all times. Yet she faced that pain with grace
and courage. Even the medical professionals who treated her noted how
different Sara was. Tabetha, her nurse for her last two years, said, "As a
health care provider, I expect to go in and make a difference in someone
else's life. But Sara made so much more of a difference in mine. Her
pain was just a part of her story." Most of us will never experience
chronic pain the way she did, but Sara's decision to praise God and
choose joy despite the reality of her pain is a lesson for everyone who
faces any kind of struggle, disappointment, or heartbreak.*

❧ ❧ ❧

Any time I got hurt when I was a little girl, I would go to my dad crying about my ailment and he would always do the same thing. He would take my pinched finger or other such hurt and say, "You know what the good thing about this is, don't you? It's a long way from your heart."

Then he'd laugh while trying to get me to laugh and think about anything else but my hurt. Being a kid, I would always take that sore finger, hold it to my chest, and say, "No! See? It's right here by my heart!" But the conversation and the laughter usually distracted me enough, making whatever had been hurting suddenly not so bad.

I eventually understood his lesson behind the distraction, that no physical ailment could change my heart. That every hurt would pass and I would still be the same on the inside regardless of the outside.

I've had many opportunities to put that saying to the test in my adult life, and I've realized something about Dad's theory. Some hurts aren't actually a long way from my heart. Some hurts reside there. But they don't change who I am inside. They don't change my faith. Every lesson I learned before remains the same after. Nothing is different. God is the same. Love is the same. No matter how much my heart hurts.

$$\vartheta \quad \vartheta \quad \vartheta$$

Whether a pain is close to your heart or not, it still hurts. And one person's pain doesn't diminish another's. Though Sara was in intense pain almost constantly and though she'd lost enough to keep her busy mourning for the rest of her life if she'd chosen, she never rolled her eyes at someone else's struggles, even if they could be perceived as less than Sara's own pain. She said, "I'm not bothered when someone gets a paper cut and complains about the pain. Paper cuts hurt.

Friendships aren't a competition, and the levels of pain don't matter.
Pain is pain."

    People often were curious about Sara's perception of matters
relating to pain and looked to her for insight and wisdom—or
sometimes even validation for their feelings. She was quick to share
what she'd learned and what she believed, encouraging her friends
and blog readers to look past their own circumstances and find
the joy in their situations. When a blog reader asked which type of
pain she thought was worse, physical or emotional, Sara responded
thoughtfully, weighing both sides and pointing us all back to faith in a
God Who creates beauty from everything, even pain.

϶   ϶   ϶

I was asked recently which is worse: physical pain or emotional pain. I have to say, though I obviously understand physical pain, I probably empathize more strongly with those in emotional pain because emotions often leave us with less ability to choose our reactions than physical pain does.

Even when physical pain doesn't fade, I'd still choose it over emotional pain. The big ones—betrayal, judgment, intense loss—they can immobilize the spirit, which is more limiting than physical immobility. That being said, both types of pain are inevitable. And both types of pain are ones that can make us grow stronger if we keep ourselves focused on the One Who knows all, sees all, and loves us through it all.

I haven't had a break from pain in years. Mine fluctuates between really awful and wanting to beat my head against the wall until I'm unconscious. In other words, I have chronic pain. It is torture and exhausting, but the emotions that come with it are what make it harder.

It's the dread of having to wake up the next day, if sleep is even possible. It's the grief over a life that was dreamed of and lost. It's the anger over stupid decisions to do things I know I am incapable of but attempt anyway. It's the sadness of being isolated and alone. My emotional pain, derived from the physical, can be more paralyzing than the fact that I can't move from the couch.

I'm not diminishing the physical. It can literally make me feel like I'm losing my grip on reality at times. But the physical causes the emotional, and that takes an exhausting toll. It's when my mind is able to align with my heart so I can make the choice to smile that I start coping. It's only with faith that my emotions are in check—and only then can I deal with the physical hurdles in front of me.

Both types of pain bring growth. And that growth, in the end, is the thing we often wouldn't trade. When people say they can't see the good coming from the pain, my answer is that it's not our job to know. It's God's. It's just our job to trust, whether we see it or not, that He brings beauty from the ashes. And maybe the beauty won't show up in my life. Maybe it will bring beauty to someone I'll never meet. My job is simply to trust Him. To go through the physical and emotional pain and embrace the peace of knowing that He is taking care of it. It's not about how bad the pain is. It's about how good our God is.

♥ — ♥ — ♥

Sara never wanted her relationships or conversations to be about her, much less about her pain. She didn't want to be an imposition or to worry anyone, though she wanted to be honest, too. "Like everything in life, I suppose, it's about finding a balance. Some way of being honest enough that they trust I will always do my best to tell them the truth, and being tough enough to put on a good face so they don't worry so much. There's a certain amount I can't hide from them. Sometimes it's obvious I'm sick; you can hear it in my voice and breathing. Or when a pain jolts and there's nothing I can do to stop the reaction in

my body. But I try to smile and keep talking, to make eye contact so
they can see I mean it when I say it's okay."

Sara knew it was hard for her friends and family to see her in pain
and worked hard not to draw any attention to it, but it was still jarring
to see. Her friend Matthew describes seeing Sara's pain: "Sometimes
while telling me a story or while listening to me gab about something
silly or meaningful, a sharp shooting pain would dart through
Sara's body and she'd lunge forward and scream out. And then she'd
apologize for screaming. It didn't matter how many times we told her
to stop apologizing, she never did. A year or so ago, the pain started
getting worse. And she started having long periods of time when she
struggled to breathe. She'd run out of breath. She'd lunge forward in
pain, gasp for some air—then keep right on talking like that's what
everybody did."

Something about pain—the shock of our bodies or our hearts
crying out indignantly, desperate for relief—creates a deep desire for
control in most of us. As Sara dealt with both physical and emotional
pain around the clock, she constantly cycled through feeling the hurt,
wanting to control it, and releasing it back to the only One Who is
truly in control. That became even more challenging as her health
and abilities continued to decline, changing rapidly and forcing her to
adjust daily.

9 — 9 — 9

I've been learning to go with the flow, while at the same time
trying to will the flow to go in my direction. It's a recurring topic
in my everyday life. As much as I've learned to adapt to what life
is handing me at any given moment, I am also constantly trying
to figure out the rhyme and reason of it all.

If I hit a wall of exhaustion, I'm trying to figure out if it's the
weather or something I've done differently that day. If my pain is

greater than usual, I go over my medications in my head to make sure I didn't miss something, and then retrace my steps to figure out when I could have overdone it.

Lately, I've had a nerve problem in my leg. I know in reality that the pain in my leg comes from a nerve that has pressure on it from the inflammation in my spine. I know in my head that there is no rhyme or reason to the inflammation or the pain. The nerve pain is constant in a certain part of my leg. It's either tingling or itching or deadened or filled with little stabbing needles. I'm used to all of those.

The part I'm never sure of is when the lightning will strike. When a bolt of fiery lightning will shoot into my thigh and drop me to my knees in pain. It can happen when I'm perfectly still or when I'm moving. It can happen multiple times an hour or just once a day. It can happen when my body is in its normal state or when my pain is elevated. It's an equal-opportunity annoyance, and there's only one thing I can do about it.

I can go with the flow. I can accept it for the inconvenience that it is, deal with it when it arrives, and move on when it goes. There's no use anticipating its return; pain operates on its own schedule. So I've decided not to worry about it when it's gone and just enjoy a lightning-free moment when I can get it.

My body has given me no choice but to accept that, so I do. But I am realizing that's how I should be handling most things in my life. Because, like it or not, we have no control over most things in life. Most things are going to happen whether we worry about them or not. Most things can't be handled ahead of time, but are only able to be dealt with in the moment. Most of our free time is wasted trying to make something happen that can't, or trying to avoid something happening that's inevitable.

That's been one of the benefits of being sick for me. I've learned to take life as it comes, when it comes—rather than anticipating life's next move and wasting precious time worrying about a future I have no control over.

ꝯ — ꝯ — ꝯ

Even when dealing with increased pain, Sara held tight to her sense of humor. If she admitted to her blog readers that she wasn't feeling well, she'd almost always follow up that statement with a joke about understatements and being called Captain Obvious. She acknowledged that her situation could seem simply ludicrous at times, that experiencing infections or complications from medication on top of her "normal" pain was outrageous. Yet she rarely succumbed to self-pity, leaning toward humor and hope so much more often.

After feeling the effects of a thunderstorm one summer, she wrote this tongue-in-cheek letter on her blog:

> *Dear Rain and Thunderstorms:*
>
> *As much as I love the sounds you make, and the way you make me wish I were back home at the farm listening to you while reading a book under the tin roof of our patio, you are hell on my body. It's like having a good-looking boyfriend who can sing, but then he makes you run fifteen miles uphill at a dead sprint at six in the morning every day. Sometimes the pretty just ain't worth the pain.*
>
> *I love you a little less every year,*
>
> *Sara*

Sometimes, though, the pain was so severe even Sara couldn't find anything to laugh about. When those times came, her preference was to work through the pain and her own reaction, process it all and figure out the lesson to be learned, and then share it with her blog readers. But when the steroids she took for pain and breathing began to cause her serious problems—and eventually Cushing's disease—her friend Nicole urged her to share her life as it was unfolding.

❧   ❧   ❧

My friend Nicole gave me a (loving) talk the other day about the fact that, in my disdain for complaining, I actually never talk about my life in the present tense at all. And she's right. (Don't you hate it when that happens?) So here goes.

I have been sick the past three and a half weeks simply because I left the house. I have to tell you, I was prepared for it to be rough but I had no idea how bad my body and its reactions had gotten.

In addition, the steroids and breathing treatments and other meds I take have a lot of side effects for me, which means I have to really just go with the flow of the moment. The most obvious side effect is that I now so closely resemble the Stay Puft Marshmallow Man from *Ghostbusters* that I'm waiting for offers to star in the remake. I've expanded so quickly that at some point every day my skin actually aches. Add on the shakiness, the sleeplessness, the exhaustion that fights the constant feeling of being antsy, the hot flashes, and the weird feeling of a slight vibration all through my body all the time, and you have the parts that I can learn to live with.

It's the other stuff that has made this hard. Because of my disease, I have gone off and on steroids a lot. And because of my disease, it takes larger doses of steroids to take care of the problems. We try to not stay at the higher doses for longer than absolutely necessary because each time I go on and taper off, the rebound pain that comes afterward is more intense. So, after the two-week mark this time, I tried a small step-down of the steroid. My lungs weren't great, but I wanted to see if the small change would make a difference or if they would stay stable. Two things happened. One, my lungs didn't stay stable. Two, my body went insane.

The next morning I woke up to a lot of pain in my knees and I could barely hobble behind George (my walker) to get to my meds. It got better after I took the steroids but never went away, and would intensify before my next dose. It wasn't fun, but it honestly didn't alarm me; weird pain happens to me all the time so I stayed at the lowered dose that day.

Then the next morning I woke from a dream where I was screaming in pain, only to realize I really was screaming in pain. I had waves of pain from my hips to my toes and struggled to get up and out of bed, only to put my feet on the floor and discover I couldn't put pressure on my legs. I couldn't walk. The pain was too much and my muscles wouldn't hold me. I got myself to the walker and sat on it, pushing myself on the walker to get my meds, all the while in more pain than my brain could process. It seemed to take forever and, in a word, it sucked.

I took my meds and waited for them to kick in and quickly realized that I should not have decreased my steroids. Yeah, I catch on quick like that. So I'm back on a higher dose and take it during the night as well to make sure it stays evenly in my system. I am, admittedly, dreading what will come when my dose changes, but whatever happens I will be thoroughly informed of what to do by my doctor and will be ready.

The reason I'm telling you about this is that so many have e-mailed to ask how I am and what is happening here, and I feel like I owe you the truth even if I don't like how that looks. And I don't like how it may worry you. And I don't want you to feel bad for me. I'm also telling you so you can understand what I mean when I tell you that how I feel changes frequently throughout the day and makes writing consistently a bigger challenge than usual. But you should know the first thing I want to do in my moments of strength is to sit at this keyboard and type for a bit, even if it did take all week to put together this long post. And it's lovely for me to know that you're still out there when I do.

9 — 9 — 9

It doesn't take mind-numbing pain or the loss of our freedom and abilities to send many of us straight to complaining. Even if our aim is to lean on God and endure whatever He's given us, sometimes it can be tempting to slip into martyr mode rather than truly accept our circumstances with gratitude and joy. When that happens, pain becomes even stronger because it pulls us down into suffering. Sara recognized this temptation and resisted it—but only with God's help. Enduring so much physical pain for so long gave Sara the opportunity to really consider its connection to her emotional state—and she realized that one didn't have to react to the other. Choosing to trust God in the midst of pain rather than fighting and lamenting is a lesson we can all benefit from learning.

9 — 9 — 9

Pain and suffering are obviously closely related. But I don't think they have to go hand in hand, because the physical can be separated from the emotional. Not all the time. Sometimes it's a process, but when we are open enough to step out of the way and let God fill it with His presence, it's a whole different ball game. And it requires us to trust with everything we are.

Pain is a constant part of my daily existence. I honestly can't remember what it was like not to feel every joint in my body. I walk with my walker in my dreams, and when I have a dream where I'm outside, I'm usually panicking and asking someone how I can get back indoors before I stop breathing. It's just who I am now. My friends have gotten used to the fact that I wince and utter, "Ouch," and sometimes stop talking mid-sentence when the pain makes me catch my breath. I barely notice I'm doing it. I'm so accustomed to the pain now that I don't consider it suffering as much as I used to.

But there are physical moments when the pain causes real suffering, moments when it escalates and is unrelenting to the point of making me sick. I physically suffer. But when I let Him, God fills me with His presence in my spirit, and I can feel strong in the middle of that weakness.

Emotionally, a hole can be dug inside us so deep that it seems everything good has been excavated from our lives. We all have different ways that happens. I've lost abilities and freedoms and the potential for many things. You may have lost someone you've loved or found yourself in situations you never dreamed of facing. A pit is dug—and despair is the first visitor that wants to knock at your door.

It's in those moments that I pray for God to get me out of His way. It's in those moments that I stop praying for what I want and start praying for Him to change my heart for what He wants. I pray that I can be aware of His opportunities. It requires me to trust Him completely. That doesn't change my physical pain. It doesn't change the loss. It doesn't improve my earthly situation. But it does change the suffering.

It allows me to choose, and rather than answer the door to despair I can instead invite His presence into the pit. That pit looks jagged and deep, but it turns out to be a God-shaped hole in the center of our beings. A hole that is dug by circumstances and choices is filled with His grace.

I am in pain. He has made sure I don't have to suffer.

9 — 9 — 9

At times Sara's disease seemed like a cruel April Fool's joke. As soon as she processed and adjusted to a new loss or kind of pain, she would

*be faced with another. Her body seemed to plot against her, constantly
attacking her in new ways. Sara was a little kinder to her body and
simply called her immune system ignorant. Still, though her disease
was like a painful carousel she couldn't stop, Sara insisted on seeing
the gifts it had given her and the way she'd grown as a result of going
through each stage. Every person who met Sara could see that she was
in pain. But every person who met her also saw that she was being
refined and made more like the God she loved.*

〜 〜 〜

My friend Len recently gave me a book called *Where Is God
When It Hurts?* by Philip Yancey. It was interesting because it
actually talked about pain from a medical standpoint, and then
went on to talk about ways of dealing with it, looking at it, and
helping others through it when you are the one who is well. There
weren't really huge revelations in it for me, but there were a lot of
head-nodding moments where he put into words things I believe.

One of my favorite quotes from him is this: "We are not put
on earth merely to satisfy our desires, to pursue life, liberty, and
happiness. We are here to be changed, to be made more like God
in order to prepare us for a lifetime with him." Whether we like
it or not, being changed sometimes means living through painful
circumstances.

For years, I struggled with the way I looked. I went through
treatment for anorexia when I was sixteen, and while I ebbed
and flowed in that recovery over the years, the one thing that
never changed was my internal dialogue. I was so sure that if I
could just control how I looked, I would be happy. It was a facade
of control that I was sure was the answer to every bad feeling I
ever had.

Slowly, over the years, as I got sicker and my body failed me,
that false control slipped further and further from my grip. I was

on and off steroids, the weight I so carefully controlled spiraling in any direction based on medications and hospital stays. Yet, as it all went haywire, I still believed that I would get control of it again.

Once I got off the steroids, my weight would stabilize. Once they controlled my pain, I would work out again. Once I got control of the circumstances in my life, I could arrange my future the way I envisioned it.

It's amazing how much credit I gave myself. I believed that somehow, even though it was medically impossible, I would be stronger than this degenerative disease.

Then Cushing's happened. I went from my well-controlled small frame to just shy of two hundred pounds in a matter of four months. And I had to find a way to live in a body I didn't recognize. I had to find a way to be joyful in a state that was my worst nightmare. I decided I was just going to have to learn to live in this body that I couldn't stand.

But in the next breath my lungs were infected and my body was getting sicker. In the next breath my dad suddenly died and the shock mixed with illness sent my body into a spiral that in mere months had me losing all the weight steroids and Cushing's had put on my frame.

Now I'm back to where I started. Below the weight I was at when Cushing's hit. And what did all of that craziness do for me? It changed me.

Through the hardest times in my life, I stayed open enough to learn my greatest lesson: control is an illusion. Life will do with me what it pleases, my circumstances will change, my pain will fluctuate, my finances will come and go, my health will alter at will (and alter my weight right along with it), and the only thing I can do is stay open to letting God change me in those circumstances.

He used the circumstance of my life to help me grow. He used those circumstances to change my heart. We are here to be changed, to be made more like God in order to prepare us for a lifetime with Him. And more often than not, being changed hurts.

I've come to understand that the only thing I can control is whether or not I open my heart. Open it to embrace my circumstances. Open it to be who He needs me to be in the here and now rather than assume happiness can come from the "If only..." and "When I get..." Open it enough to let Him in to change me here so I can be with Him there.

4

Resting Quietly on the Heart of Jesus
On Dealing with Fear

⤳ ⤳ ⤳ ⤳ ⤳

It is such folly to pass one's time fretting, instead of
resting quietly on the heart of Jesus.

—St. Therese of Lisieux

*As Sara's disease progressed it became clear that she would not get
better and that she would undoubtedly get worse. For someone already
enduring unfathomable pain and loss, that diagnosis could have been
terrifying. But rather than be paralyzed by fear, Sara chose to trust in
the Lord, knowing that no matter what disease handed her, God was
in control and giving her strength. Though we won't all be confronted
with a diagnosis that promises a lifetime of difficulty, all of us face
uncertainty and challenges that scare us at times. Sara's approach to
handling the proverbial monsters under her bed can teach us all about
trusting God and choosing Him over fear.*

⤳ ⤳ ⤳

I used to be afraid.

When I was little, I had such a fear of something happening to my parents. I would wake up from dreams of them dying or disappearing, unable to fathom how life could exist without them. What would I do? Where would I go?

I worried. I wondered. I let fear overtake my dreams.

Mom would sit on the bed and tell me they had no plans of ever going anywhere. She'd tell me she was healthy; she'd remind me of how strong Dad was and that if he could lift me and throw me above his head, he was certainly strong enough to conquer just about anything else that came his way. I figured that made sense. Besides, she was my mom. I trusted her. That's really all it took.

When I got sick in my twenties, that fear crept back in. Not of losing my parents this time, but of losing my life. I wasn't afraid that I would die, but that I would get to a point where I wouldn't really be living anymore.

I knew how hard it was to cope with the pain and the changes this disease was bringing into my life already, and each time I would do a little research, trying to become informed and ready for whatever lay ahead, I would read about how much more could happen to me.

The progression of ankylosing spondylitis is different for everyone. Not everyone becomes disabled, not everyone has all of their systems affected, not everyone becomes like I am today. But I knew it could happen because I had read the stories.

Once again, I was afraid. But this time, so was everyone else. The look of fear that flickered across the faces of those who loved me when they asked how bad it could get simply reflected the fear on my own. No one knew the answer. I still don't know the answer. I only know what I'll go through when I go through it.

And going through it has been scary. I have been afraid. But one day, the thought passed through my head that if I really trusted God, if I really believed that He cared about every hair on my head, I had nothing to fear. Regardless of what would come into my life, He would make sure I was well.

I had an image of myself, standing on a beach with the water lapping against the shoreline. I pictured a line being drawn in the sand and I knew in that moment I could choose Him, or I could choose fear. But I couldn't choose both; they couldn't coexist.

I chose Him. I chose to believe in God just as much as I believed in my mother's words when I was a scared little girl. I chose to trust Him.

Recently, I've been asked by many people how I can do that. How can I trust someone, even if that someone is God, when I know that He could have spared me from all of this? How can I trust a God Who allows hurt to happen when He has the power to take it all away?

My answer is that God fixes what is broken, and I trust Him to fix my broken places. But you can't fix what isn't broken.

I don't believe God did this to me to teach a lesson or to prove a point. There are many reasons I could be sick, and Him inflicting this on me isn't one of them. But I do believe He didn't stop it for a reason. Life breaks us sometimes. We have the free will to make decisions that will break us. Other people have the free will to take actions that will break us. Genetics can play a role in making us sick, and that can break us.

I have been through things that have broken my life. And I trust Him to never leave me there. He is the Father Who will pick me up when I am fallen, broken, hurt, tired. And He is the Father Who fixes me in those broken places. He fixes my spirit, my heart, my sadness, my loneliness. He brings joy and peace and refuge so I am stronger now than before I was broken.

He watched the pieces fall apart, but only so He could put me back together the right way. When life happens and I feel like things are falling apart, breaking into pieces, I just remind myself that He can't fix what isn't broken.

This year, God took fear off the table. It's finally very clear: fear isn't an option. When He drew that line and said fear or Me, and I didn't choose fear, it was one of those fundamental changes where I know it's no longer an option. Everything can be taken away, and I trust Him. Period.

This change is total grace for me, because getting rid of fear wasn't a specific thing I was consciously trying to do, although it definitely fits with the intention of how I'm trying to live. Something shifted in me and I know that I unequivocally trust Him.

That doesn't mean life is suddenly carefree and easy. It means that in the midst of hard stuff, I'm not scared. If I look back on the past year there is no doubt I'm doing worse now than last year. But I'm not afraid of what next year will bring. He took that option off the table. And I intend to work as hard as I need to in order to keep it that way. I can't know what happens tomorrow. But I know He's got it under control—and that fear is off the table.

9 — 9 — 9

Though she leaned fully on God after He took fear off the table, Sara admitted that worry got the best of her before any sort of doctor's appointment. Thankfully she'd found a caring, knowledgeable doctor, but she still worried about describing her new symptoms clearly. She was afraid that when the time came, she wouldn't be able to put her pain into words for the person who could possibly help her. But, as she said later, she should have known better. She should have known that God would provide exactly what she needed when she needed it.

9 — 9 — 9

Recently I watched the television special on Randy Pausch and his famous talk "The Last Lecture." For those who haven't heard of him, Randy passed away from pancreatic cancer, but shortly after being diagnosed he gave a talk to his class at Carnegie Mellon University about the lessons he has learned in his life. I had originally heard of him because of this speech and, like everyone else, was incredibly inspired by this man. But while watching the interview last week, I actually found myself more drawn to the sensibilities of Randy's wife.

As Diane Sawyer interviewed her, she spoke a lot about finding acceptance and the mantra she repeats to herself when she feels as though it's all too much: "I have everything I need." I was drawn to her because that is what I say to myself daily.

My friends and I use the book *Traveling Light* by Max Lucado for our faith sharing group. Each chapter focuses on a verse from Psalm 23, and chapter six stood out to me with this verse: "He leads me beside the still waters." Seems like a simple statement, but Lucado focuses on the fact that God leads. He doesn't push us into something and say good luck. He walks ahead of us and tells us where to go, where to turn, how quickly to walk. And in order to do all of that, He gives us all the direction and help we need when we need it. I trust that He has it under control, and my job is to walk where He leads, to not be distracted and miss the opportunity to be a servant to Him through the circumstances in my life.

I guess it's the epitome of living in the moment. I choose to trust that God is going to provide me with what is required of me when it is required. At times I would like Him to supply me with what I need ahead of time because it's hard to face the unknown. But I have to have faith and trust in His perfect timing. The opposite of that trust is worry, so when I begin to worry about my present, my future, my life, I stop and remind myself that I have everything I need. I never know where I am going, and I have never felt less in control in my entire life. And it is true freedom.

I really don't worry too much in my life anymore. The one time worry tends to get the better of me, though, is when any sort of doctor's appointment comes around. A visit to my main doctor, Annie, is the exception to this rule as she is the kindest, most thorough and caring soul I've ever met. But specialists of any kind tend to get the better of me and my nerves, thanks to experiences with doctors who have been impersonal, quick to judge, and dismissive.

So when waiting in the doctor's office last week, I reminded myself that I have everything I need. And in the end there were no new medications for me to try and no great changes in store for my day-to-day living, but I had the words to describe my pain and symptoms to my doctor when I needed them. And he listened as I needed him to. He was worried about my lungs so he got me to the allergist across the hall for a consultation right then. I had what I needed. When I needed it.

A passage in Hebrews says, "We will find grace to help us when we need it most." I trust that. Even when I don't feel it, even when worry creeps in, I choose to remember that I have everything I need. And I promise you do, too.

ϑ ϑ ϑ

Sara loved words and just as she was intentional about how she lived, she also was careful about how she communicated, about choosing words to describe her life and her heart. So when she wrote about "fretting," rather than just calling her experience worry or fear, it was purposeful. And that word carries a weight others would not.

When I think about the times I've experienced frightening or otherwise overwhelming situations, I have to admit I don't stop

*at the worry stage. More often than not, I progress pretty quickly
to the whining stage and the it's-not-fair stage. Faced with the
inconveniences and injustices of life, I fret. Though fretting doesn't
change a thing about my circumstances, it sometimes feels necessary,
like something I just have to get out of my system. And I don't think
I'm alone in this.*

*When your house won't sell because the real estate market crashed,
when your manager takes credit for the hard work you put in and
the success that resulted, when your spouse doesn't get the transfer
or promotion, when your brother dies in a senseless accident, when
a friend stops talking to you over a simple misunderstanding—how
often are you unable to move on until you've stomped your foot just
a little bit? Amazingly, God is big enough to handle our shaking
fists and protests that we just don't understand, but He's also patient
enough to wait for us to stop our foolish fretting. After getting seriously
sick simply from opening a window on a warm day—and realizing
that she would likely never leave her house again—Sara knew
something about fretting.*

9 —— 9 —— 9

I love this quote from St. Therese of Lisieux: "It is such folly
to pass one's time fretting, instead of resting quietly on the heart
of Jesus." It makes me take a deep breath and get my mind in the
right place. But it also sometimes slaps me upside the head and
reminds me that I've been spending too much time fretting lately.

Fretting is a vicious cycle, isn't it? Part of me thinks it's okay.
I've earned the right to fret a little, haven't I? I went patiently (for
the most part) through this past year, taking my lumps as they
were given to me. I stayed inside all of last summer, feeling sick
each time I attempted to open a door or a window, because of my
reactions to the air. I didn't step foot outside of my home from
July until March, knowing that if the air didn't get me, I would

certainly fall on the ice in those winter months. Not to mention the fact that everyone and their dog was sick, and I was trying to avoid pneumonia this year. It was just too risky to try to leave these four walls.

But I really didn't fret (much). I was patient—but I fooled myself into thinking it was because I was being trusting. What I didn't realize at the time was that my trust had conditions built into the fine print. I figured I could make it through a year indoors because I was certain once we had a good freeze, whatever weird thing in the air was bothering me would be killed off. I knew if I just waited again until spring I would be rewarded with fresh air and sunshine. I was sure.

I was wrong. And now I can't stop fretting.

I'm trying hard not to. I'm trying so hard not to stomp my feet and throw myself on the ground, kicking and screaming into a fit of unfairness. I'm trying not to yell into the nothingness that I don't deserve this. I'm trying so hard not to face the fact that I'm not going to ever sit outside in the fresh air, feeling the warm sun on my skin and watching as the silent breeze rustles through the hosta plants. I'm not going to sit on my patio reading while my dog snuggles up next to me, content with keeping one eye on the wrens in their birdhouse to make sure they aren't taking up too much of his turf. I'm not going to wield my new camera while sitting in a friend's yard, taking pictures of their kids and of the flowers, with the sunshine streaming through the lens.

I have to let go of those images that simply aren't meant to be a part of my daily existence. And it sucks. I just can't pretend that it doesn't.

But—and there's always a but—if I really trust my God, if I really believe that He loves me beyond condition and holds me gently, then I can't stay fretting. And I really do trust Him. I really do believe. Which means I need to keep stepping forward in faith and remembering that there is plenty of joy right here within my four walls.

It's not easy, but the only way I know how to move forward is to let it out and then let it go—and I'll start by resting quietly on the heart of Jesus.

Sara had amazing self-discipline. She may not have been able to resist a Sonic slush or one more episode of Alias, *but most of the time she kept her thoughts in check. Left alone with our own thoughts for just an hour, many of us might get a little crazy, succumbing to insecurity or anxiety—but not Sara. She was honest about the times it was a struggle, but after years of practice, trusting God and choosing joy truly had become second nature for her.*

Resting quietly on the heart of Jesus became more challenging when she realized she had no choice but to reduce her steroid intake, a process that would bring mind-numbing pain. She had to do it, and she knew God would hold her through it, but facing it was hard nevertheless.

I'm not usually afraid of the unknown. I realize I can't anticipate or prepare for something when I have no idea what may be coming around the corner. The problem arises when I know what's coming, there's nothing I can do to prepare for it, yet I know enough to anticipate it.

As each day has passed this week, I've gotten sicker. I've gotten weaker, more dizzy, more tired, more nauseous, more pain, more everything. The past two days I have struggled just to sit up and stay awake. What this tells me is that the doctors are right: I have got to get off these steroids or the Cushing's will keep getting worse.

That's the rock. Here comes the hard place. The last time I tried a small reduction of the steroids, I woke up the next morning in more pain than I knew how to handle. It was ripples of sharp pains going down my legs from my hips to my toes, with my hips, knees, and ankles feeling like someone was tightening them in a vise. I was stuck in bed, unable to walk or move for about three hours while I waited for the medications to kick in. That day I increased my steroids back up to normal, and despite the increase I still woke up the next morning and experienced the same pain, only it lasted five hours. Yes, five hours of biting-a-pillow kind of pain.

So you see my dilemma. I have to get off the steroids or I keep getting sicker. When I try to get off the steroids, the pain is insane. This is where I wish it were unknown, because right now I can't help but anticipate something I know I can't do anything about.

Tomorrow I'm going to start a steroid reduction. And it's a bigger reduction than the last one I tried. And unlike last time, at some point I have to bite the bullet and stay at the reduced dosage if I'm ever going to get off of these things. The part I know is what it will be like the first day or two because I've already been through that a couple of times. However, since I've never stuck it out past that point, the unknown is what will happen when I don't increase the steroid dosage back up.

Rock, let me introduce you to Hard Place. We're all about to become very good friends.

There's a part of me that is resolved and ready to just get on with this. And there's a part of me that would run far away if I could. But that's the thing about illness...there's nowhere to run. There's no taking a break or a breather or a vacation. There's only walking straight ahead into the storm and trusting that God will find a way to get me to the other side of it.

So, not to be overly dramatic or anything, but tomorrow I'm walking head-on into the storm. And while I know you all pray for me all the time, and I am so grateful for that, this is the first time I'm asking for you all to pray for me. I don't think the pain should get too bad until Monday, but after that I have no idea what will happen or how we'll proceed. I have home nursing at my disposal, but mostly I just need for my doctors to know what's best for me and I need to have the strength and fortitude to do what needs to be done, no matter how painful or scary it is.

❧ — ❧ — ❧

When I think of the Bible verse in Philippians that says, "I can do all things through Christ who strengthens me" (Philippians 4:13, NKJV), I think of Sara's steroid reduction. Surviving that took a strength that no person possesses, but God held her—and strengthened her— through it. As she finally began to recover and return to a new normal, Sara's family and friends breathed a collective sigh of relief, thankful she was no longer in that kind of pain.

Sara knew that her life with chronic pain and illness would continue to be a roller coaster, though. She admitted that something new was always around the corner, but she joked that at least that meant she'd get a good rush once in a while. What didn't give her a rush—or the fun kind, anyway—was playing a mental chess game and attempting to predict what would be around that next corner. She struggled to balance the awareness that every single decision she made could have long-lasting or even permanent ramifications with her determination to trust God. Although most of us don't suffer from a life-altering disease the way Sara did, our choices have consequences, too. And it can be hard to find a balance of both living intentionally and trusting God with our lives. Sara's response to an avalanche of "what if" scenarios can help us navigate our own roller coasters.

❦ ❦ ❦

Last week we tried to add another pain medication to my current regimen. We'd done that with a different med before Christmas, and I wound up reacting and very sick to my stomach over the holiday. In retrospect that just seems inconvenient, because the reaction I had this time was something I couldn't have imagined.

It involved literally not being able to move for hours, not being able to call for help, and when I finally could move I got hives, my skin itched and burned, I was shaky and sweaty, and my heart pounded so hard my chest hurt for days. My voice and breathing are still wonky. It was scary and painful, and I feel like I'm a very lucky girl to have come out of it.

But the major point of this isn't the story of the reaction. To me, the ramification that matters is never being able to try a new medication again. When the nurse arrived we both agreed I wouldn't make it through a reaction like this a second time, and that means the only medications I can have are the ones I'm currently on.

That's a daunting concept when you're only thirty-seven years old and you know you have a lot of years ahead that could get a lot worse.

Although I've never been smart enough to learn how to play chess, I imagine living with this disease takes the same strategy. People who play the game say they are always trying to think three moves ahead to see where the game could take them.

For me, every decision, every action has future implications. We look at the fact that every new medication for my disease has caused reactions, which have increased in severity. We know that nearly every time I've gotten very sick, like with pneumonia or Cushing's, my body has taken to attacking a food I regularly put in my system, like whey or cocoa.

The point is this: If I get sick and another reaction occurs, it could involve my body reacting to a medication already in my system instead of food. If that happens, I will have absolutely zero options for controlling the disease or the pain. As my nurse and I were talking, my brain started to spiral thinking how bad the pain would get if I ever reacted to the medication that helps control the disease. It swirled as I realized there would be nothing left to do about it.

My nurse then brought up the fact that it's not out of the realm of possibility that I will start rejecting more foods. When I asked her what would happen if I ran out of food options, we started on our "chess game." We'd have to go to a feeding tube or IV feedings. But then we remembered that I couldn't keep a PICC line in a few years ago because my body reacted to it. Which means we'd have to find another option for nutrients that didn't involve a permanent access point. But a lot of supplements would contain ingredients that I wouldn't be able to ingest.

Do you see why my head starts to spin? One move, which leads to another move, which leads to another problem, which leads to no solutions because there are no realistic Plan Bs. It sounds dramatic and unlikely and like some bad Lifetime movie plot, but the truth is that it's very possible in my world. I mean, I'm the girl who can't breathe normal air.

That's when I had to stop and remember something very important: God gives us what we need when we need it. Not before. Not after. But during.

So many "what if" scenarios could realistically happen to me. But I can't plan ahead and expect there to be solutions to problems I'm not currently facing. Because God gives us what we need when we need it.

Never once in my life have I been faced with a problem when an answer didn't present itself in some form or another. And if God hasn't abandoned me in thirty-seven years, I don't know why I think He would abandon me in the thirty-seven yet to come.

So I'm quitting my chess game before I even learn how to play. I'm going to trust Him. And praise Him. And go along for the ride. I will not let fear have the power.

Over the years Sara learned many lessons about her faith and herself. Some lessons, though she understood them well and even shared them with others, were harder to internalize—and remember.

I don't know about you, but through my entire adult life I've been fighting the same battles, learning the same lessons—over and over again, until I wonder if I'll ever learn, if it will ever be easier to trust God, to ignore the lies of perfectionism, to control my temper. But even Sara knew the nature of our humanness, and she was humble enough to share her own lessons as they played on repeat in her life. "Apparently, it's the same lesson just being looked at and learned from different angles," she said. "And it always comes down to trust."

"I just hate feeling so helpless." A friend texted me this a few weeks ago. I had a lung infection that wasn't improving and it left us both feeling in the same boat. The helpless one. Without a paddle.

For me, it was a month of frustration and hitting my head against a brick wall. For her, it was years of watching me go through it and knowing there was nothing in the arsenal of "say or do" that would change a darn thing.

I texted her back something I had honestly never thought before, until the words had escaped my fast-moving fingers: "I feel helpless, too. But maybe I just need to remember that I'm supposed to be helpless. I'm not supposed to have control over it."

And suddenly I believed what I had just written. I felt a bit of relief and let God take the burden off of my shoulders. That made sense, since my shoulders weren't where it was ever supposed to rest in the first place.

I realized a long time ago that worry was a result of not trusting God, and I drew that line in the sand and chose God over fear and worry. Anytime it would creep in I would literally stop and remind myself that God has never left me alone and was not about to start now. It was time to do that with feeling helpless, too.

Oh, don't get me wrong. I still feel helpless. But that's not such a bad thing anymore. Instead it's a burden released to the One Who can shoulder it for me. I'm not fighting the feeling of helplessness because it no longer means that I'm weak, that I need to fight harder, that I need to figure out the riddle when there is no real answer.

No, when I feel helpless now, I am strangely comforted by the fact that it's not my job to figure it out. I can find strength in being helpless because I know that God is the One in control of it. Not me. Not my friends. Not even my doctors.

He knows what to do. He knows how to handle it. I'm just along for the ride. My only job is to trust Him. And I can do that.

5

Giving Up and Letting Go
On Expectations and Goals

There's an important difference between giving up
and letting go. —Jessica Hatchigan

*Sara wrote quite a bit about how her disease forced her to redefine her
life's goals. She made it clear that she wouldn't have determined these
purposes for her life without her disease. She pointed out that her new
and improved goals were just that—a better version of the life she
wanted to live rather than a lesser, second-place version of life.*

I'm starting to think that life mainly consists of learning to
accept things we say will never happen to us. I'm sure you have
your own examples. I have friends who swore they would always
work but now love being stay-at-home moms. I have friends who
were sure they'd want to stay at home with their kids who would
go crazy if they didn't have a job outside of the home to challenge
them. A good friend of my family got married, and both he and

his wife are successful doctors who never wanted kids. They are now captivated by their three beautiful boys. Life takes us by surprise, and we learn to embrace what is meant to be, rather than what we meant to create.

I had all sorts of plans. I was sure I would work as a writer, I would get married and have kids, and I would love cheering them on through their lives. I would be busy and active, involved in my church and my community. I would have dinner parties and card clubs and fill up life.

The day I had to quit working I remember telling a friend that even harder than letting go of the dream was knowing I wouldn't be a productive member of society. I had to learn to let go of the picture of my life that was in my mind: the husband, the kids, the home with the parties. And I went from saying what I would do to declaring what I would never do.

I wouldn't stop doing freelance work. (I did.)
I wouldn't let pain stop me from pushing through physical
    therapy. (I did.)
I wouldn't rely on a cane. (I did.)
I wouldn't go on disability. (I did.)

I wouldn't . . . well, it doesn't matter how many examples I give because determination only takes a person as far as their body and situation will allow. The latest thing I've had to embrace, despite my most emphatic declaration over the past few years, is a walker.

I would absolutely not get a walker. (I did.)

Of course, I had no intention of relying on a walker. I was simply going to get something that had a platform of some sort so I could get my laptop from one room to another. Walking with crutches obviously makes carrying anything difficult. I was able, for a long time, to walk with one crutch and carry a drink or a plate from one room to another, but it was getting harder to keep my balance doing that and with the sudden nerve pains I became unstable easily. So there I was with wireless Internet and no way to use it because I couldn't move the laptop to a comfortable chair.

Then I found the "rollator," which, by the way, I really need to find another name for. Because while I like the fact that I don't have to call it a walker, I think *rollator* sounds like something that old *Saturday Night Live* character would call it. You know, the dude who changed everyone's names so (for example) instead of calling me Sara he'd say, "The Sara-nator!" Quite frankly, I'd rather call it George.

But, as usual, I digress. I had gotten to the point where I realized I needed it for a carrying function, but I was still resistant. I even called my friend Susie to see if she would talk me out of it. She's usually all about saving money so I told her what I was thinking, assuming she'd think of another way to get a laptop from point A to point B without spending a dime on a contraption. I called the wrong girl. Apparently she had been rooting for a walker for a while but had been afraid to bring it up because she thought I'd get mad.

She was right: I really didn't want it, but I bought it. And now I seriously don't know how I managed before I got it. It helps me get my computer into different rooms and has a basket for my camera (and, as my mom suggested, my Lifeline button). But more importantly, it's taken away my fear of falling. I'll admit it: I'm finding it pretty darn handy. George and I should get along just fine.

9 — 9 — 9

I was one of those women Sara mentioned who swore she'd never be a stay-at-home mom. I couldn't even fathom giving up a career for days filled with craft projects and Sesame Street. *No one was more surprised than me when I decided to leave my job to stay home with our three-year-old daughter.*

Around that same time I was coming to terms with breaking more "I'll never" promises, most of them related to my weight and clothing size. When I decided, as a brand-new, highly motivated stay-at-home mom, to clean out and organize all the closets in my house, putting my small(er) pencil skirts and button-up shirts in the pile for Goodwill was harder than I'd expected. Those clothes represented a part of my life that I'd left behind, at least for the time being, and parting with them took a whole lot of resolution (and produced a whole lot of tears). Reading Sara's words about her own closet reminded me of this experience. As her mobility and abilities were limited further and further, she realized she no longer needed many of her favorite clothes. But while I knew that weight loss and a second career were possible for me, Sara knew she was closing the door permanently on a life that required cute dresses and clutch purses.

➳   ➳   ➳

Two nights ago, tornadoes ripped through nearby towns, tearing apart homes, families, livelihoods, and security. Today I spent hours going through my closet and putting together things to give to the people in one of the towns. In the process of searching for things that may help rebuild their lives, I discovered myself finding a way to let go of my own past life.

Before I became sick I took my full life for granted. I assumed I would always be social, rarely at home, singing at weddings and working to my heart's content. My disease has taken those plans from me, but I hadn't been able to let go of all my hopes just yet. Now because of the need of others I finally let go of the dresses I don't need for singing at weddings, the shoes with heels that are too high to use with crutches, and the little clutch purses that can't swing hands-free across my body.

They haven't been of any use to me for such a long time, but I couldn't seem to get rid of them without a reason. I mean, what if, after ten years of getting worse, I wake up tomorrow able to sing at a wedding again? What if, after barely leaving the house a handful of times in the last year, I break out and go on a date? Those heels would come in handy.

But the reality is that I have to let go of sifting through my life just as the people in those neighboring towns will soon have to do. They're going to have to step aside and watch the bulldozers carry away the remnants of their old lives so they can start rebuilding their town, their homes, their families, their livelihoods. They will find their new normal in the midst of the chaos and see blessings in tragedies. They will struggle between holding on and letting go—and I will cheer them on in spirit as I do the same with my life.

Somewhere in the midst of all of their trouble, in my heart aching for them and my trying to imagine their loss and their gratitude and their hope, I let go of hopes that aren't meant to be fulfilled and offered the material remnants of my past life for their new lives. It's another start, and a fresh start always means hope is on the horizon. Theirs may be the hope of building bigger, stronger, better. Mine may be the hope of building a resiliency for the pain that lies ahead. But both are hope nonetheless.

⁓   ⁓   ⁓

The first time I visited Sara we sat, along with her friend Alece, on her couches and talked and laughed and cried for hours. We talked about her family and Alece's ministry. We shared ideas and made plans. We talked about favorite television shows, and Sara gasped in shock

when I told her I had not watched a single episode of Friday Night
Lights. *But mostly we talked about my career and my dreams, and my
frustrations with both.*

*I remember getting in my car to drive home that afternoon and
hanging my head. I'd come to visit Sara, to show her love—but
she'd spent the whole time asking about my life and listening to me.
I can't say that's the first or last time that's happened; I'm a talker,
that's for sure. But in that case I realized that our visit had gone
exactly the way Sara wanted it to. One thing every one of her friends
mentions when remembering her is how much she loved listening to
her people talk about their lives. They mattered to her, and she wanted
to hear it all.*

*Sara was an incredible friend, but she also understood what it was
like to have dreams of doing meaningful, interesting work—only to
watch them slip away. She knew how it felt to come to grips with a life
that was completely different from the one she'd planned and hoped
for. She knew the hold that expectations can have on a person's life
and heart, and she knew how God has a way of changing it all when
you aren't expecting it. My career path may have felt twisty but hers
had reached a dead end. Her understanding that the end of one dream
leaves room for the beginning of another, better one taught me a lot—
even if I do still talk too much.*

𝄢 𝄢 𝄢

I used to work at a magazine. I had goals back then, about
what I wanted to do professionally and how I wanted my life
to turn out. But the way I look at goals changed when my doctor first approached me about applying for disability. Maybe
"approached" is the wrong word. I was sitting in a hospital bed
(it was one of the three times I was in the hospital that year)
with my laptop open, typing up dictation from an interview I
had done so I could write an article. I'm sure you can imagine

the look on her face as I was working while hooked up to an IV of antibiotics and a Demerol drip. Work was not what she had in mind for me to be doing! Recovery was more important at the time, but I was still in the mode of fighting to maintain a life that had already changed. My mind just hadn't caught up to the reality of it yet.

I would say Annie (my doctor) looked surprised, but I think *disapproving* was more the word for it. How in the world did I expect to get better and fight off an infection when I was expending all my energy working? That was happening in that hospital room, but it was the pattern my life had been following for a while. As soon as I started getting better after being sick or experiencing a pain flare, I'd resume life as normal. And that normal would wear me down and start the cycle all over again. When I finally applied for and was approved for disability, I had to figure out what my goals in life were now going to be. And eventually I came up with this:

Life Goals:
1. To not be ashamed to stand before God.
2. To fulfill God's plan by living the best life I can with what I am given.
3. To be aware and present in every moment.
4. To love what I have and not yearn for what I lack.
5. To spread the joy, not the fear.
6. To be intentional in all things.

Later, when I was doing less and less freelance writing as my health deteriorated, but hadn't yet discovered the world of blogging, I knew I still needed a way to maintain my creative side. So I took the doors off the closet in my spare bedroom, stuck a desk in there, and renamed it an "alcove." (Because, you know, *alcove* sounds much fancier than a *desk in a closet*.) Then I did something that would have gotten me in a heap of trouble when I was little: I began writing on the walls. It's one of my favorite spaces in my home. While everything else in my world is organized and in its place, this little alcove is whimsical. It's the place where I wrote all the sayings I loved, inspirational quotes I wanted to surround myself with—reminders of who I wanted to be and how I wanted to live my life.

And that really was the key. I no longer had a career, I was stepping closer and closer to being homebound, I had no husband or children or potential for my life to change. I had to figure out who I wanted to be, outside of the ways most of us define our lives.

I wrote my list of Life Goals on that wall, reminding myself that my goals weren't things I could "do" or "accomplish." They were goals for how I wanted to live in my spirit. It's a list we all should sit down and make—and a list I wish I had made when I was well and able-bodied. So far I haven't had a situation come up in my life that hasn't been covered by these goals. They're how I want people to remember me, the impression I want to leave on people I meet.

They are lofty goals. They're not easy to reach every day. But they are what I was left with when I took away the idea of having a career, having a family, having financial security or some sort of status in society. I think it's something I had to look at, but it's something I should have been looking at all along.

9 — 9 — 9

Sara loved inspiring quotes, words placed together in a way that could delight our souls and move our hearts. She wrote them on her walls, and she painted them on canvases. She doodled them on cards and shared them in blog posts. But more than anyone else's words, the statements that sustained her when life was at its most difficult were her Life Goals.

Sara's Life Goals were touchstones, her mission statements, and reminders of what she'd chosen as most important for this life. As she became more limited physically, she questioned her purpose, wondering what she could still do that would make a difference. Her Life Goals came in handy more than ever during those times, bringing her back to a focus on living the life God had given her, on loving what she had and not yearning for what she lacked.

ᕗ   ᕗ   ᕗ

I've been feeling antsy lately. Unsettled.

Part of it is simply because I can't get comfortable. When I'm still, everything inside my body feels like I should move, but when I move, everything about me screams to stay still. Moving hurts and stirs up more problems. But being still hurts, too, and nausea comes with either option. So it's a never-ending battle between being still and being in motion.

It's a push and a pull where neither satisfies. And it creates an antsy feeling in my spirit as well, because I'm stuck between being still and being in motion with life, between the desire to do everything and the ability to do nothing.

I lie in bed, in the antsy stillness, and think of graduations approaching. I think of friends' birthdays and anniversaries and kids soon to be romping in the summer sun. I think of thank-you notes to write, e-mails to send, canvases to make, phone numbers to dial, and ways I could bless people. Ways I could help. Ways I could be present.

But the stillness trumps it all. I lift my arms to grab the card and the air escapes my lungs and I am too tired to rise. I go to grip the pen that will write the note and it shakes like I'm eighty years old, wondering where the old familiar motions have disappeared to. So I think of the people in my mind instead of on paper, and I whisper a thank-you in a prayer for them and pray they feel the love from where they are.

I wonder about my purpose, what that might be if the things of my mind and heart can't be produced by my hands or my lips. I wonder what I'm supposed to be doing if I can't do anything. I'm seeking the answers in outside things—in activities and achievements—that I can no longer do or accomplish.

And I am still. And antsy. But then I think of the quote reminding me of the difference between giving up and letting go. And I realize that part of seeking out what my purpose is, what my goals should be, how to fulfill what God has put in front of me, is to let go.

Let go of the ideas that I can't make happen. Let go of the expectations I put on myself to be more than myself. It's a constant process as I lose more abilities, to adapt and adjust and let go of the notion that what I should be is anything other than what I am.

It's a fine line, between giving up and letting go. Because I'm not giving up on having a purpose. I just may have to let go of putting energy into the things that no longer work so I can focus my energy on the things that still do work.

And I realize that in some ways I'm lucky, because my life forces me to be still, be slow, let go of the externals so I don't lose sight of my purpose.

ꝫ——ꝫ——ꝫ

Just like anyone going through a struggle, Sara sometimes didn't realize how much her life—and her heart—had changed over time until something made her stop and think. She liked to say that "habit makes able," meaning that by simply choosing the right steps over and over, we eventually can do those things we once thought impossible. As she looked for the gifts in every situation and chose purpose every single day, Sara created habits that eventually changed her completely—even down to the magazines she wanted to read (although nothing could break her celebrity gossip habit!).

❧ ❧ ❧

The reality of just how different my life is was brought home to me in the oddest way recently. A good friend of mine asked me if there was a magazine I would like to have a subscription to. Because I'm so mature and all, my first thought was a celebrity tabloid. But since I check People.com every day already, it seemed like a waste to duplicate.

As I thought of magazines I've read in the past, I realized they didn't fit me anymore. I used to love working out, so I read fitness magazines like *Shape* and *Self*. That wouldn't work for me now. Getting magazines about sprucing up my house or the latest clothing trends and jewelry didn't make my heart go pitter-pat anymore, either. Those things still interest me, but there's a part of me that knows I'll envy those people flitting about in their cute clothes while going to a movie or lounging in the park. It's just not my life anymore. I can admire it, and I can appreciate it when other people are experiencing it—but it's no longer me.

That's when I realized, for sure, that something had changed inside of me. After all those years of hearing people proclaim that it's not about what you do, it's about who you are, I finally, really, fully understand that. I had to lose my job, my health, my abilities, and my hobbies—all the things that made me "who I was"—to see who I am.

No magazine can define me or identify with me anymore. There's not a magazine that can tell me how to dress, or how to decorate. Not one can tell me how to work out to achieve my best body or how to find the man of my dreams. What I have and what I value can't be found in the pages between covers.

What I've found is that I'm resilient. I've found that I have fortitude and faith. I've found that I care more about your feelings than mine. I've found there is nothing that cannot be redeemed and there is no one who doesn't need encouragement. I've found I don't need to be who the world wants me to be, because all the world really needs is who I already am.

The truth is that life in my thirties is no better or worse than I wanted; it's just completely and utterly different. The wisdom comes in knowing that it is exactly as it should be. The joy comes in learning to live it, not despite all I've lost, but because of all that this life has brought to me.

ᵍ ᵍ ᵍ

As someone who writes and speaks about the dangers of perfectionism, I know this particular struggle is not uncommon. Many of us spend too much of our lives striving for a level of excellence that's unattainable—and then have a hard time dealing with a house that's less than clean, kids who aren't always well-mannered, and the inability to juggle career and ministry and children and husband without dropping one—or all—of those balls regularly. Thankfully, I've gotten a pretty good grasp on the fact that the world isn't perfect and life isn't fair, and managing those expectations has grown easier over the years. But as so many others have found, when it comes to what I'm capable of doing, no such logic prevails.

Sara didn't struggle with the heightened level of perfectionism that some of us do, but she still fought disappointment when she couldn't do as much as she wanted to, as much as she thought she should be able to. The unexpected death of her dad took a serious toll on Sara's health, and as she struggled to work through her grief and her illness, she got fed up with herself. This time she wasn't frustrated by unmet expectations of life, but of herself.

❧ ❧ ❧

This weekend was a hard one for me. I find myself getting so frustrated with myself sometimes. I am frustrated that the grief takes over so hard, when I know Dad is in perfect joy and we are so grateful for having had him in our lives. I am frustrated that I'm so tired, that I'm still getting sick every day, that I'm not bouncing back like I think I should. I am ashamed that it has been three months since Dad left and I still haven't finished my thank-you cards. Heck, I've barely started them.

People, I'm even frustrated that I can't finish my dog's haircut. It was Riley's poor grooming that brought this to light for me. I was telling my friend Shannon that I was pretty sure animal control was going to come rescue him if I didn't get him prettified pretty soon, that I had barely taken a brush to the poor pup, let alone scissors to his mane, since Dad died. And that's when she gave me a little perspective.

She asked me when I'd had time between grieving Dad and trying to be there for my family and getting sick every day and dealing with the migraines and the pain and wishing I could be outside and getting infections and rashes and staving off pneumonia and reacting to every other thing with which I come in contact.

She reminded me that living and breathing and moving are my job. And they can be stressful. She reminded me that my life is incredibly slow, but it's my harried mind that needs a break. She pointed out that I need a Sabbath from myself.

I can't take a Sabbath from my life. From my pain. From my grief. From my circumstances. But in my mind and heart, I can try to learn how to give myself a break. A breather. A rest from my own frustrating expectations.

I think our expectations of what we want life to be often overshadow the good things that are already in front of us—and that's when we miss the silver lining. When my sister was going through a divorce, we were on the phone talking about hard decisions and out of my mouth came these words that I would later cling to for myself as well: "All God asks of us is to live the best life we can with what we are given." We are all given different blessings and different crosses to bear, which means we can only take care of what's in front of us in that moment and do the best we can.

I don't know if that sentence brought any relief to my sister, but as my life changed over the years it proved to be something I needed to hear. I needed to remind myself that my old gifts were gone, and they didn't serve me in living my best life anymore. I had new gifts and crosses given to me, and I had to rethink how to live my life with them. It took a while to find my new normal, and that continues to change daily. But when my focus is on living the best life I can with what I have in that moment, I always find my silver lining. I'm not expecting what I used to have or what I think I should have. I'm looking at the blessings right in front of me and saying thank you every day.

6

Rainbows and Rain

On Wanting What You Have

❧ ❧ ❧ ❧ ❧ ❧

If you want the rainbow, you gotta put up with the
rain.
—Dolly Parton

One of Sara's Life Goals was, "To love what I have and not yearn for
what I lack." Every person faces the discrepancy between dreams and
reality, and learning to love the life we have makes all the difference
in our outlook and attitude. Sara's life and choices teach this lesson
beautifully.

That doesn't mean she looked at her present circumstances and
potential future with rose-colored glasses. On the contrary, she often
contrasted her "before" and "after" lives. But while anyone else would
look at a young woman in her position with pity, grieving all she'd lost
and would never regain, Sara looked at her reality and called it good.
She truly believed that her life—the homebound, pain-filled, isolated
life—was infinitely better than anything she could have dreamed up
or created. She truly believed that she was blessed and refused to be
moved from a place of gratitude and joy. And then, because she knew

how unusual that perspective was, Sara shared it with anyone who would listen or read. We didn't have to wonder, "How does she do it?" because she told us every chance she got, fulfilling another one of those Life Goals by spreading the joy.

⋟ ⋟ ⋟

I remember the first time I really understood the parable of the vineyard workers. I had heard this Bible story all my life, but it finally clicked in college.

In Matthew 20, Jesus is recorded telling the story of a man who needed help with his harvest. He hired some men for the day, telling them the day's wage, which they accepted, and they began working. Throughout the day, he realized he needed more help to get the work completed, so he went out multiple times and hired more workers. Each time he offered the wage to his new workers, they accepted and set out to work.

At the end of the day, he called all the workers together and paid them the same day's wage. It was the wage he had offered to them, the one they had all accepted. But the men who had worked all day in the fields were angry. They said they were being cheated because they had worked harder and longer than the others, and should be paid more than those who had worked only the last few hours.

In reality, the problem wasn't the amount they were being paid for the work they'd done. He gave the workers what had been promised to them. The problem was in the worker who only felt cheated when he compared his life to someone else's. The problem arose when the worker took his eyes off of his own mission, the one he'd agreed to gladly—and decided he wanted the easier task that had been promised to someone else.

I have to remind myself of this story because it's hard for me not to feel cheated. It's hard for me to be thankful on a holiday weekend when I have to be alone in this condo. When there is no bustle of family or friends, when I can't enjoy a turkey dinner, when I have no one to talk with and laugh with and reminisce with and grieve with. It's hard when I compare my isolated existence with what I know is happening everywhere else.

But that's not the deal I made with God. I promised Him my whole life, and He promised He would love me, never leave me, and take me home to have eternal life in Heaven someday. It was the wage He promised me, the wage I accepted—and it's only when I take my eyes off that promise that I feel cheated. God is honoring His deal. It's me who looks at life and says, "I'll have what she's having, please."

Does going back to that Bible story make all the hard-to-deal-with feelings disappear? Of course not. It's still brutal. But it reminds me of what I believe. I believe that God has a purpose for me, and that my job is to be faithful to whatever comes with my life. I will do my daily task and honor Him as I believe He is honoring me.

I believe it. Even when it doesn't feel good. Even when it hurts and is lonely and feels unfair and requires me to grieve a life I was never promised.

Bottom line, people: I am filled with joy. I'm exhausted, I'm in pain, I'm just getting by. But I am so incredibly blessed. I have a lovely home, an adorable pup, family and friends who care and people who love me, not despite my disease but because of who I am. I am blessed because I take nothing for granted. I love what I have instead of yearning for what I lack. I choose to be happy, and I am. It really is that simple.

I've heard that faith is believing without seeing. I think it's also believing without feeling. It's believing in those moments when our hearts ache and our tears betray us by spilling over when we know better but feel the pain anyway. Having faith is not about always being in the happy place, as much as I try to live there. It's about believing even when the happy place isn't ours to have. It's about those times when we can't see or feel the promise, but we believe in the promise anyway.

Faith isn't a feeling. It's believing despite our feelings. And I do.

ഴ   ഴ   ഴ

Sara liked posting on her blog daily, but she sometimes worried about running out of things to talk about. She joked that after she listened to her friend Kelly talk about her day during a phone call, Kelly asked about Sara's day, and after pausing to think about what she had going on, she said, "Well, I showered today and Riley peed on the floor." Of course, leave it to Sara to make even the mundane entertaining!

Between her creative spirit and her determination to savor her moments and find beauty in the ordinary, Sara never bored or disappointed the blog readers who came to her site to check on her, to spend time getting to know her, or simply to soak her in. Still, she wanted to make sure people found value in her writings and decided to answer readers' questions in a regular series she called "Blog Peep Questions." One week she answered a question from her friend Susie, who asked if Sara ever got irritated or hurt by hearing about her friends' and family's "little" problems or everyday events.

ഴ   ഴ   ഴ

One of my Life Goals is to love what I have and not yearn for what I lack. That decision is one of the reasons why I am never hurt by hearing about Susie's day—or anyone else's. They don't make me yearn for what I don't have, but instead I love what I do have through them.

The other reason is that, while I may be physically differ-ent, I am emotionally the same person. Nothing in life makes me happier than when other people are happy. And nothing will stop me in my tracks faster than someone who needs my ear to listen. If everyone stopped telling me their happy moments, I wouldn't have that joy in my life. I truly and sincerely live vicariously through each and every success, joy, piece of gossip, and video of their kid's concert that they bring into my world. Just ask my parents! When I talk to them on the phone and they ask how things are going, I regale them with stories of my friends and their kids and their lives.

Because sharing in what is happening with them *is* what is going on with me.

Megan, my friend Kelly's daughter, used to call me and play her piano recital pieces over the phone. I would answer, the piano would start, and I'd sit and listen for as long as she played, and then tell her how amazing she was. When she did that, I got to be a part of something outside of my life. When Suz tells me about the hectic morning they had or tells me funny stories about her day with the kids, she makes me a part of her life.

And my friends, by complaining when they stub their toes or telling me about the fun night they had going out to dinner together, they let me know they wish I were there. They make me feel like me—the same person I was to them before I was sick, the one who listened and gave them advice and laughed with them and cried with them. Of course I long to be with them in all of those moments, but hearing about it and feeling as if I were with them is the next best thing.

$$\vartheta \quad \vartheta \quad \vartheta$$

While people start blogs for many reasons, Sara's blog truly was for the people, and she opened herself completely to those who visited every day. No question was off-limits, and so from her favorite ice cream flavor or what superpower she'd most like to whether she would trade the lessons she'd learned in her life for good health, Sara's blog readers asked—and she answered.

♪   ♪   ♪

I wouldn't trade what I've learned for good health. It sounds insane, even to me, as I sit here in pain, but I can say it without hesitation.

I really, really would like to be in good health. I'd love to walk outside, sing to my heart's content, dance, go to a friend's house, travel home for the holidays. I'd love to not have to think through every single movement I make and I'd love to be blissfully ignorant of the word *debilitating*.

But more than all of that, I love feeling at peace, believing, trusting, accepting, and being open to life as it is. And when it comes down to it, I don't want to trade fulfilling whom God needs me to be for my own comfort.

People used to tell me they prayed for my healing so I could be whole, but the only thing that would make me less than whole is if I chose what I needed over what He needed from me.

Whole. I have fought this word a lot in my life. So many truly well-meaning people have used the word in order to tell me what I could be.

If I would just take another remedy.
If I would just pray a certain prayer.
If I would just... <u>fill in the blank</u>.

If I would just do any one of the magical things that they have just heard about from their aunt's cousin's mother, then I would be... wait for it... WHOLE.

I couldn't figure out for the longest time that what was hurting me was people looking at my life and viewing it as something other than complete. To them, I was less than—less than perfect, less than their idea of what I could be, less than I used to be, less than I should be. It took a long time for me to sort through all of the noise and clutter of it all to realize that I am whole.

I am in pain, sick, frail, homebound, bedbound, without great possibility or potential in my future. But in all of that, I am whole. I am complete. I am exactly what God made me to be in the exact time He created me to be it. God made me as I am. To do exactly what I am doing. And I am whole.

Of course there are moments when I long for a more "normal" life. I'd love to have a husband and a family, a career and a social life. I want to be a part of things—a real, tangible, active part of the outside world. But the truth is that I have no idea who I would be right now had all that happened. I have no idea what my priorities would be, where I would have lived, what friends would be surrounding me. God set me on this path and lined it with blessings. I can't presume my dreams would have turned out better than His plans just because they seem easier in my mind.

If I judge my life against others'—or even against the life I used to have—if I'm grading myself on a curve of normalcy, then of course I feel shortchanged. But being normal is not the goal. The goal is to live the best life I can with what I am given.

Obviously my life is intensely abnormal compared to others', and these past few months have been the hardest of my life. But I still wouldn't trade it for the normal one I always thought I would have, because this is the one He meant for me to live. It's a relief to know we're not graded on a curve, but instead loved for exactly who we are designed to be. I am whole. I am who He created me to be. And I wouldn't want to be anyone else.

"I have everything I need." Sara said that—and meant it!—all the
time. That made it hard for friends to send her gifts, by the way. But
she wasn't trying to be difficult. Sara truly was content with what she
had. If pushed to pick her absolute favorite things, though, she picked
moments, every time (in addition to frozen Oreos and Friday Night
Lights' *Coach Taylor). "Moments are my favorite things," she said.*
"Moments can't be taken away or broken or replaced. They can only be
given. Moments are now officially my favorite things."

୨ —— ୨ —— ୨

I was watching television the other day when a commercial
for the Iowa lottery came on. It showed people receiving boxes
at their homes that glowed with a bright white light and said
DREAM across the side.

The actors would jump and scream and run in the house yell-
ing, "Honey! I got my dream!" It was fun and exciting, and it got
me thinking: what would be my dream? I realized that I don't
have one. I don't have a tangible, money-driven dream that the
Iowa lottery would be able to deliver for me. And I realized it's
because I'm full.

I sat here for the longest time and tried to think of something I
really needed. Or even something I wanted really badly. And I'm
not saying this to be all holier-than-thou, but I really have everything I need. Even before I was gifted a new bed for my birthday,
the one thing I needed to be comfortable every day, I'm not sure I
would have thought of it as a wish. Because I just feel full.

I woke up this morning and Riley was waiting for my eyes
to open so he could lay his head on my stomach and I could
pet him until I could move. It was a moment of being truly full
because I was needed and wanted and not alone.

I have a safe home and a comfortable place to lay my bones all
day. I have friends who call and e-mail. I have a community of

people who really see me. I have family members who love me and check in on me and I am full. I have everything I need.

I worried about it for a minute, because we live in a world of goals and dreams and five-year plans. But as much as I would like for some things to be different in my life, I think I like this lesson I've learned in the way my life turned out. God has given me everything I needed as I've needed it. And I am full.

Sara was full, and she was whole, and she was content in the life God had given her. But the reality is that some days were full of bad moments—of pain, disappointment, frustration, loss. And in those moments, Sara was (mostly) thankful that she'd taken the time to write over the years, saying "out loud" what she believed and what she knew to be true. She mentioned more than once that she hadn't even realized she thought something until she'd physically typed it in an e-mail or blog post. Those moments of awareness, along with deliberate explanations of her understanding and perspective, moved her and sustained her.

The positive thing about blogging is that I write down what I believe so I can look back and remind myself how I want to handle things. And the negative thing about blogging is that I write down what I believe so I can look back and remind myself how I want to handle things.

You gotta love a good double-edged sword in those moments when you'd rather pretend you don't know better. Because there are times when I am hanging on by my fingernails over here. Seriously.

I've been asked if I ever just throw up my hands and say, "Enough!" or cry uncle or some other more colorful exclamation.

The answer? Oh my soul, are you kidding me?! Yes, of course I get so tired of living like this! Sometimes it will hit me that, for the rest of my life, I'm never going to get a break. I'm never going to get a vacation from the pain and the tired and the constant effort. I won't ever have a random "What the heck, I'll just open a window" kind of day.

I do my best to live in the moment because the moments seem to change in a breath. Living in the now is the best option. But every once in a while, when all my moments have the commonality of intense pain, and all the changing breaths have the commonality of new issues, I find myself wanting to live in the land of I-Don't-Wanna. You know, that mystical land that allows us to throw a fit somewhere deep down inside when we are too old to throw one on the outside.

The weather keeps changing and the storm fronts keep moving in and the dizziness and nausea and pain won't subside. And I get weary.

But I still know better. I still trust Him. And I still have all my blog posts reminding me who I want to be. I can be weary. I don't have to like it. But I do have to keep believing.

For me, it helps to have a plan. Most of this past week I spent more time in bed than I did on the couch. (Yes, sitting on the couch is my goal right now.) But I keep my sanity with certain cozy blankets that make me think of the people who gave them to me, certain movies ready to go in the DVD player, my computer propped on the bed, books and notebooks on my side table.

I make lists of the things I want to try to get accomplished eventually so that my brain isn't always stuck in the unpleasant present. But I never put anything on the list that I know could be unattainable, because that will just frustrate me later. I keep my meds across the room so I have to get up and move whether I feel like it or not, because it's good for me. I keep things around me that remind me of the joy, of the good things in my life, of the blessings that the pain can't touch if I don't let it.

It's not always the big things like pain and immobility that can rob us of our joy. Sometimes it's just the tedious repetition of the day. But we still know better, we still trust Him, we still keep believing—and it's so much easier to do this when we have a plan to keep ourselves in the middle of the joy.

❧ ❧ ❧

Sara's plans for holding on to joy included returning to Scripture and her Life Goals and the words she'd written. But sometimes to hold on to her joy, she had to let go of other things. Though she'd donated some of her clothes following a nearby tornado, Sara still had a closet full of cute clothes she loved but knew she'd never wear again. While she could have held on to them and reminisced about the good times she'd had in them, she chose to do the hard thing—and give them away.

❧ ❧ ❧

Sometimes we get lucky and joy just knocks us upside the head. It's cozy and comforting and we sometimes take for granted that it will always be available and waiting for us at the end of a hard day. But more often than not, joy is hidden in the cracks, in the unforeseen places God builds into our hardest times.

When I discovered that being homebound was going to be a permanent lifestyle for me, I gave away some things that I knew I wouldn't ever use again, things like purses and coats and dresses. This summer, though, I looked at my summer clothes and realized what a waste it was to have them sitting in my dresser. They didn't fit, but they also felt like a reminder of all the places I'd worn them, and all the places I would never go again. Sure, I could have saved them to wear around my house, but that thought didn't bring me joy. It's like all my past fun times of going out with friends in those cute clothes suddenly got confined to my house with me.

Reality is that life is different. And when I look at a closet of outfits that scream, "Wear me somewhere fun!" it causes me to long for something I'll never do and places I'll never go. In those moments, with something as simple as clothes in my closet, I find myself longing instead of living. Wishing for what was instead of what is. Fighting for a life that is no longer mine.

I didn't want to do that—so I asked Susie to come over to go shopping. I could have just given her boxes of clothes and been done with it, but I honestly want to squeeze joy out of every little moment I can. I miss shopping, helping other people pick out clothes, figuring out what outfits they could put together from their closets. So I made Susie try on every single piece of clothing and we talked about them just as if it were a shopping trip. And I had fun. Giving brought me joy. Shopping in my own house for someone else brought me joy. Later, when Susie would tell me she had worn something of mine out to dinner with friends, it brought me joy. It made me feel as if a part of me were still there with her, still having fun, still participating.

That joy was sitting right there in my drawers. It could have brought me sadness and longing, but instead I chose joy. I put the work into something sad and made it happy.

It's something for you to think about as you go through your day today. Stop and take in your moments. Look at them from another angle. Joy is sometimes in the most unlikely places. You just have to put in a little work before you can find it.

༄ — ༄ — ༄

Sara found so much joy in giving Susie her old clothes—and forcing her to model them in a fashion show—that later she gave several pairs of shoes to her mom and her stack of jeans to her sister. And yes, she enforced her "must put on a fashion show" rule for them, too.

⸱ ⸱ ⸱

While some girls hoard purses and others have closets lined with shoes that are to die for, my obsession has always been jeans. I love me a good pair of jeans. The Buckle and I have been very good friends. When I tell you that my closet still had stacks of jeans lining the top shelf, I'm probably downplaying it. And this weekend, as I looked at Laura, my cute sister who I knew would probably fit into the majority of those jeans perfectly, I decided it was time to let them go.

She didn't know about my rule at first: if you take my clothes there must be a fashion show. I like to pretend I'm shopping and help decide what is cute and not cute. I told her what to wear with which pair, which ones look great with boots and which ones need a fantastic heel. I taught her about good pockets that make good-looking tushes and which kinds of stitching make a girl look slim.

I loved it. And did it with a happy heart. But I was holding one stack back: the stack of my favorites. The cute trouser jeans that are perfect for the date that isn't casual but isn't dressy. The jeans that give you a little extra confidence when you walk in a room. The pairs that represented the moments I loved and wished I could have just one more time.

I know it sounds crazy, but that one stack of jeans kept me longing instead of living. And Laura saw it on my face. She said they could be my "in the event" jeans—in the event I could ever get out and do those things again I could have them back. It was sweet and kind, just like my sister. But it wasn't real. So I took a deep breath and said, "No. They aren't 'in the event' clothes. I have no more events. And that's okay. They are yours to wear and take me with you. That's how our life works now."

And that took us from a fashion show to facing our new reality. Suddenly my family is faced with a world of "never" rather than a world of "someday." I'm never leaving these walls again as long as I'm on this earth. We are never seeing Dad again as long as we are on this earth. We are never going to be given back those moments we loved to live just one more time. And that hurts more than words on a page can convey.

But we also have a world full of living to do on this earth, and that can't be done if we are pretending our lives didn't change. The only jeans in my closet now are a few that hold no meaning. They are just ones to slip on if I feel well enough when friends come to visit. Because my reality is that most of the time when friends visit now, they have to sit in bed with me because that's where I am, in my comfy yoga pants, most days.

The reality is that we are going to have Thanksgiving and Christmas and birthdays without Dad. But we still have them together and we need to live and celebrate those moments we are still given. I could long for the husband and children I always dreamed of, or I can live in the families I have created with people who have blessed my life. I can wallow in the missing or I can live in the present, with sweet memories I can carry with me.

Just as Laura will carry me with her while wearing her cute · new jeans.

9 — 9 — 9

Sara, who preferred to call herself optimistic, strong, and hopeful, could also be called stubborn. Like all of us who are more strong-willed than the average bear, that spirit served her well at times and not so

*well at others. But when it came to her faith and her choice to live fully
and joyfully, Sara's determination and focus were inspiring to all of
us—stubborn or not.*

> — > — >

Every day I awake to a sameness and the unexpected all at
the same time. I wake with the same intentions, the same goals,
the same disease, the same feeling of wondering how I will fill
another day in the same position with the same issues. And every
day I face the unexpected—the changes in the intensity of pain
and the areas of pain and the unknown side effects of pain.

Every day I face the consistent schedule of taking my medications, but the unexpected schedule of what fills the in-between
moments. The moments when I find out if goals can be met. The
moments when I may be able to type and return e-mails or I may
not be able to do more than lie in one position and fight to rest
while being too restless to sleep.

But all of those are externals. They are just what happens
to me. They are not me. Because every day is also beautifully
chosen.

In the midst of the aching sameness, and the achingly unexpected of the external, is the beautifully constant of the internal.
The things I choose. The joy. The bliss of a new room. The happiness of a view that now includes birds and chipmunks and even
pesky raccoons. The joy of technology and friends at my finger-
tips, and the overflowing e-mail in-box that I can't keep up with
but is full of everyday hellos I can't live without.

Every day I choose the one consistent internal ability that I
know will never be taken from me. The one that feels like my
purpose. The ability to love people by praying for them. Like
clockwork I go through my people, I pray for them, I ache for

them, I grieve with them, I rejoice with them. And I praise Him through all of it.

Every day, in the sameness of good and bad, He is with me. I am never alone. I'm luckier than most because I trust that knowledge with every fiber of my being. Every day I get to be His and He always shows up. He shows up in the joy and in the pain, in the fun and in the nausea. He shows up. Just for me. Which means every day is a good day. A joyful day. Because I choose Him. Every single day. And you can, too.

7

Placed Purposefully

On Surrender and Trust

❧ ❧ ❧ ❧ ❧

Either we are adrift in chaos or we are individuals, created, loved, upheld and placed purposefully, exactly where we are. Can you believe that? Can you trust God for that?

—Elisabeth Elliot

Choosing joy and hope despite pain is difficult, and despite her determination to make those choices, Sara was no Pollyanna. She was honest about the effort it took, the commitment it required to continue choosing joy. She wrote on her blog, "I made a decision a long time ago that I was going to choose joy. I even painted a big rectangle on my wall and printed it in big letters so I wouldn't forget to make that choice every day. The major word in that rectangle isn't joy; it's CHOOSE. It's looking around me when life is difficult and trading every complaint I have for something beautiful in my life that far outweighs it. I know, it's that Pollyanna thing again, but living joyful beats being cynical any day of the week." Sara

indeed chose to let go of her complaints, her expectations, and her
need for control. She surrendered to God, trusting Him with every
part of her life.

❦ — ❦ — ❦

My friend Vicky asked me once, "Did you have one moment of surrender or were there several moments?" I think it's a daily process, and I think I have the advantage of growing up in a home that encouraged my faith.

I don't remember a moment when I first learned about God; He was just always a part of my world, always a part of a discussion, always a part of the routine. When I was little, Mom would wake us up by coming in the room and singing, "Rise and shine and give God your glory, glory..." We prayed at mealtime and before going to bed, observed the rules during Lent, and lit the candles on the Advent wreath that Dad made for our fireplace mantel. No one was beating on a Bible. It was just a part of our everyday life.

❦ — ❦ — ❦

When asked if Sara was always so focused on her faith, her mom,
Jane, said she was certainly spiritual and close to Jesus. She said,
"Our family was spiritual. We raised the children that way, and
Sara had a strong respect for the Church and her faith. But I asked
her where she got this deep, deep intensity, and she said she wouldn't
have it without the gift of her disease. The gift of her disease! But, you
know, she absolutely listened to Him. She truly lived her life with the
Lord."

❦ — ❦ — ❦

Of course, when you're a kid, believing and trusting go hand in hand more easily. As I got older, believing was never a problem. Trusting was a whole other story. I knew God could do anything, but as I started to be able to question and rationalize, the question of why He would spend time on little old me was perplexing. The idea that my seemingly huge junior high problems of mean girls could be fixed by someone who wasn't in the room when they were spreading rumors seemed ludicrous.

But then I got older still and started realizing that God could fix all those things. But He doesn't fix them by sealing shut the mouth of the girl spreading lies. He fixes the problem when I ask Him to fix me. I believe He can do anything. I think He can physically heal me; I think He can stop a tornado and halt a flood. But I think what is most powerful is when He lets natural things happen and lets people use their free will, and at the same time fixes my heart and spirit to handle them.

I think because I'm pretty matter-of-fact about my life, and because I seem quick to accept my fate, it gives the impression that I don't think miracles can happen. And that's not true. I believe in miracles, and I believe in healing. I believe in a God Who is so much bigger than I can imagine Him to be that anything is possible. I also believe that sometimes healing must not be what He needs for us, or it would happen to everyone.

Because God is so big, so out-of-the-box for me, I have no interest in making my life into something that wouldn't serve Him. I have had people tell me that if I had more faith I would be healed. I've had people tell me that if I just don't talk about being sick and move forward in faith as though I will be well, then healing will come from my faithfulness. I've had people tell me that I haven't been healed because I haven't told God to do it, that being timid gets you nowhere and declaring what I want will prove to God that I truly believe.

I do tell God what I think would be lovely for my life, but I also tell Him that I am fully open to whatever He needs from me. I don't think prayer is just about changing my circumstances, although sometimes it does. I think it's about letting God know I'm here, I'm paying attention, I love Him and honor Him with my whole heart. It's also about changing my heart, aligning my will with His, and asking Him to give me a heart that would rather serve Him than serve my own desires.

I would love to wake up and never have pain again. I would love to open my windows and sit on my patio or go for a walk or swim in a lake. But I don't want those things if they don't serve Him. It's really that simple. I know some people think that means I don't want it badly enough. If it comes at the expense of fulfilling a purpose He may have for me, that's probably true.

I don't think healing is about who puts their faith on the line better; I think it's about fulfilling a mission. Some are healed because that miracle will spur some on to faith. Some are not healed because that suffering will help others in some way. I'm not big enough to know which should be true for me. I trust God to make that decision. I am open to either option and I believe that if healing is meant for me, He'll make that happen.

In the interim, I'm not wasting a moment of what is by waiting for what could be. Over the course of the last fifteen years I have had progressive stages of getting sicker and developing more pain. And I have had many moments of surrender to walk through them. Just when I thought I had a handle on things, something else would happen and I would start learning to accept it all over again. Only each time, I didn't start over; I had a little more of a head start from the time before. Each time it took less time to get to the point where I could take a deep breath and say, "Okay, there is nothing that You and I together cannot handle."

❧ — ❧ — ❧

As Sara told her friend Vicky, surrendering her life to God was a daily process. To make sure she kept trusting Him, she had a few tricks she relied on. Her Life Goals and prayer life were the foundations of her daily choices, but she also used something she learned watching The Dog Whisperer. *Yes, Sara unashamedly adored her dog, Riley—or, as her blog readers knew him, Riley the blog dog. Her ten-pound white pup showed up in photos nearly every day, often on purpose as Sara captured her everyday moments with her pet, but occasionally as a photobombing puppy who insisted on being the center of attention.*

Sara wrote, "My dog loves me so fiercely I sincerely don't know if I'd be sane without him. And the truth of the matter is, having him with me all the time feels as important to me as if he were my seeing-eye dog. He is my constant, my company. He makes me laugh, brings me joy, and settles my soul." She joked that her life was so crazy her dog was on antidepressants, but the truth is that Riley was so close to Sara that he did develop anxiety over her illness. As she said, he put up her with craziness, so the least she could do was put up with his. And as it turned out, researching ways to calm down hyper dogs gave Sara a way to keep her own thoughts and emotions under control, too.

❧ — ❧ — ❧

Charles Caleb Colton said, "It is good to act as if. It is even better to grow to the point where it is no longer an act." That is how I feel this process has been for me. I acted as if I agreed with how God wanted me to act even when I really didn't. There would be times when I would lie down and think, "When do I get to have my nervous breakdown? When do I get to just lose it?" But I knew deep down that if I trusted Him to handle it, even when I didn't feel He was handling it, that it would be okay. And so step by step I acted as I knew I should, and now it's not an act or an effort.

I have always believed that once you know better, you can't pretend to be ignorant anymore. That's why my nervous breakdown never comes. I just can't pretend not to know better. I can't pretend that God isn't going to take care of me. I can't pretend that I'm not going to have what I need when I need it. I can't pretend I'm alone in all of this. I simply know better.

It's like the Dog Whisperer. (Yes, I'm serious.) When the Dog Whisperer is trying to redirect a dog's focus, he makes his *shhht* noise and gives them a tap on their chest or their back leg to snap them out of the moment. When a dog is focused, he is blind to everything but the object of his attention. The sound and the tap knock the dog's brain back into a normal state where the Dog Whisperer can then redirect its attention.

Likewise, as soon as negative thoughts start coming into play for me—like the whole "I don't think I can do this for another day without losing my sanity and grip on reality" thing—my brain gives me a mental *shhht* and it's replaced with, "You don't have to do this for another day. God's doing this for you; you just have to keep showing up."

In the beginning of having this disease, I would have to consciously stop and remind myself of the good things, remind myself that God knows what He's doing. But it eventually became an automatic *shhht* response in my head. The thought comes, the *shhht* happens, and my thought changes. I don't know if that works for everyone. I don't know if that makes sense to you, but it's how it works for me. I made a choice at some point to remind myself of the good instead of the bad, and it eventually became an automatic response.

❧   ❧   ❧

Typically Sara seized the day as much as she was physically capable of doing so. She didn't procrastinate, putting things off because they might not turn out perfectly or might end up being too hard. When she realized she needed to undergo an intense reduction of her steroid medications, however, she knew how bad the resulting pain would be—and she balked. She refused to do it, declared that she couldn't do it. Reducing the steroids that were causing Cushing's disease was crucial, though, and eventually Sara realized that resisting was just as hard as surrender. When a blog reader asked her what she'd learned through the horrible experience, she shared more about that lesson.

❧   ❧   ❧

I guess if there is one major lesson buried in that experience it's this: it takes just as much effort, if not more, to resist the inevitable as it does to go through the inevitable.

I obviously know what it's like to have pretty intense pain 24/7, but when I first tried to reduce as I normally would, it was intensely shocking to be jolted awake by a completely new and different pain. It went from my hips to my toes in waves of sharp pain, a pain that seared right down through the bone. While those waves were occurring, there was a pressure of pain in my knees like they were being squeezed in a vise that never let up.

Hence the whole "not being able to walk and falling when getting out of bed" experience. Ugh. So unpleasant.

That intensity lasted upward of five hours, and I was smart enough to immediately pop some steroids in my mouth and go back to my regular dose. What wasn't smart was declaring, "They are going to have to put me in a three-month coma if they expect me to do this reduction because I CAN'T DO IT."

Now, I'm not typically a girl who complains or throws a fit or makes such a declarative statement, but I felt in that moment that I had earned the right to tell the doctors they had lost their ever-loving minds. After all, I was the one living in this body of insanity.

But here's the problem: I knew I had to get off the steroids. I knew the Cushing's was getting worse and that it would continue to get worse as long as steroids were in my system. I knew it was inevitable, but in my mind I had decided it was impossible. I should know by now that nothing is impossible.

In the end, we changed my steroid schedule and worked on different combinations of drugs and pain meds that allowed me to put myself into as much of a coma as I could (so I guess I did get my way a little bit). Extra meds or not, it was phenomenally painful, immobilizing, and exhausting. But I got through it because I changed my attitude. I bucked up and got stubborn and decided enough was enough. I just wanted it over with. I learned that if I resigned myself to the inevitable instead of fighting it with dread, I could be mentally strong enough to handle it even if I wasn't physically strong enough.

The process reminds me of my sister-in-law, who had all three of her children without any pain medication. (Let's all take a moment of silence for that one . . .) Anyway, her second delivery went so much more smoothly than her first because she had a great labor/delivery nurse who talked her through the pain. She told my sister-in-law to stop holding her breath and fighting it, and instead let the pain be a part of her so she could breathe through it and use that to help her push.

It makes me wonder how much of our lives we spend holding our breath and fighting against the inevitable, rather than embracing the situation and using it to help us through the process. How often are we fighting internally rather than accepting the pain or difficulties in our lives? What if we could breathe through them with the knowledge that no matter the results, all will be well?

$$\text{\textit{9}} \quad \text{\textit{9}} \quad \text{\textit{9}}$$

As an artist, Sara loved experimenting with different backgrounds, fonts, and colors on her website, as well as tweaking wording, streamlining categories, and moving widgets. As a matter of fact, she was so good at creating blog buttons and other bits that people wanted to use her custom fonts and doodles on their own sites!

It wasn't just design that Sara constantly reevaluated, though. She also considered the words she used to describe herself, her life, and her blog, making sure that she represented her life—which seemed foreign to so many of her readers—accurately. More importantly, she wanted to make sure she represented her heart accurately. And when she realized that her heart had changed? She made sure we knew about it, too.

$$\text{\textit{9}} \quad \text{\textit{9}} \quad \text{\textit{9}}$$

One of the lines in my blog's About Me section reads, "This blog is about me, my life, my disease and learning to adapt to the changes life throws at all of us."

When I read it again recently, the concept just didn't sit right with me anymore. I remember typing it and believing it, but over the course of writing the blog my perspective changed greatly. To me, adapting now feels a bit like a negative concept, like God and I have different ideas about my life, and by adapting I'm begrudgingly adjusting my view rather than surrendering to His. I've learned through the trial and error of life that I don't want to adapt anymore.

I've spent the last fifteen years watching my life, as I knew it and as I dreamed it to be, slip from my grasp. I lived a number of those years fighting with all of my might to hang on to every piece I could. I adapted sparingly because I had to, but I didn't like it.

Now, don't get me wrong. Having a bit of spunk is a good thing, but the intention behind the spunkiness matters. I wasn't fighting to maintain my life because I thought it was in God's plan for me. I didn't push myself because it was in my physical or mental best interest. I fought because I was stubborn and wanted my life to be the one I had planned. I was adapting as a compromise between my desires and His. And there should be no compromising when it comes to God's purpose.

So I've changed my thinking—and it changed my heart. Just as much as I would embrace a miracle of healing with open arms, I choose to embrace all that comes into my life the same way. I've learned to embrace the pain. Embrace the solitude. Embrace the constantly changing plan of my day as my pain and energy levels fluctuate.

I've stopped trying to compromise between what I want and what I have—and I've learned instead to want what I'm given. By removing the expectations I placed on my life, I've come to appreciate the moments He's entrusted to me. It doesn't make the journey easy. But it does make it worthwhile.

There are lessons in the pain. There is discovery in the solitude. There are blessings in the opportunities that have come because of my limitations. I've learned to love hearing about what's going on in the world outside of my home as much as I loved living it with my friends.

I see every moment of my life now, both the difficult and the joyful, as a moment to be embraced. Because I know that God is in the middle of all of them. He is in the center of my storms and my blessings. He sees it all with eyes that know and understand and foresee the purpose of my situation. And I want what He wants.

So I no longer adapt, compromise, or adjust. I surrender. I simply trust that whatever is in front of me at any given moment, He is in the center of it. And there's no place I'd rather be.

9 — 9 — 9

Sara talked a lot about choosing joy and looking for the gifts in every situation, no matter how painful or difficult. But what was even more amazing was that the joy and the gifts were secondary to her. Her first priority was to obey God by trusting Him—no matter what the outcome was. And she found joy in that trust, even when her health remained poor and life remained hard. It's not surprising that trust and joy are connected, and that truth reminds me of the old hymn "Trust and Obey":

> *But we never can prove the delights of His love*
> *Until all on the altar we lay;*
>
> *For the favor He shows, for the joy He bestows*
> *Are for them who will trust and obey.*
> *Trust and obey, for there's no other way*
> *To be happy in Jesus, but to trust and obey.*

The story of Noah is one we've heard often, especially on the topics of trust and obedience. But Sara—in her typical way—had a different perspective on Noah, the ark, and the rain.

9 — 9 — 9

So many people say as they are going through a hard time that someday they will look back and see how the pieces fell together.

But I think a big part of trust is walking ahead in faith and being okay with never knowing, never understanding. I think trust comes down to walking a path simply because He has asked us to.

I thought about it as I read the old story of Noah and his ark. Everyone thought Noah was nuts. I mean, imagine it in this day and age. Imagine me randomly telling you all that I was stopping my life to build a boat the size of Noah's in my dad's field—just because I felt God calling me to.

People would be saying I had messed up my medication. People would be screaming about how the money could be better spent helping the tornado victims or paying down our national debt. People would be judging me, calling me names, ridiculing my religious beliefs, and making assumptions about my political party status. I would be a laughingstock.

Of course, we look at Noah and see that he was right. That it all worked out. That the rain came and he saved his family and God was pleased. Happy endings and hugs all around.

My question is this: would he have been less right if it had never rained? I don't think so. I think it's about saying yes without the guarantee that anything will work out in our favor. I'd like to look at my life and hope good is coming out of my disadvantage. I'd like to think that because I am remaining faithful and joyful in this situation that good things will happen for me or someone else. We can all look at our lives and say, "Well, that was hard, but look at the good that came from it."

But I think Noah was the hero before a drop of rain hit the thirsty earth. I think he said yes for no reason other than that God commanded him. And I am going to think of Noah's decision before the rain every time I have a hard decision to make. Every time I start to get weary of living a difficult life. Every time I long or wish for different.

I'm going to think of the man on dry land who said yes regardless of the outcome. Because we don't all live to see the rain. We don't all live to see the benefit. We don't all get to know if there even is a benefit. But if we really trust Him, our thirst can be quenched in the simple choice to obey, to say yes.

8

Everything Is a Miracle
On Gratitude and Praise

❧ ❧ ❧ ❧ ❧

There are only two ways to look at life. One is as though nothing is a miracle. The other is as though everything is a miracle.   —Albert Einstein

Sara chose the word praise *to be her focus in 2011. Though you can follow a thread of gratitude through all of her writings, she turned up the volume on praising God during the last year of her life. During a time when life was beyond challenging and her prognosis was crushing, Sara declared over and over, "It's not about me"—and lifted her eyes to Him instead.*

୭ ୭ ୭

I've had people asking for the past week or so about my Thanksgiving plans. *Are you having company? How are you celebrating? Will you be lonely? Is anyone bringing you a plate of their Thanksgiving feast to share?*

I'm thankful people care so much about me that they think

about my Thanksgiving, and I am so very blessed to be cared for the way that I am by people I've never even met. It never ceases to amaze me, although it really shouldn't, considering how invested I am in the lives of all of you as well.

In truth, I don't have Thanksgiving plans, simply because it's not possible. My family will be at my parents' house for a "Thanksmas" celebration, mixing two holidays into one. I obviously can't travel, and it would be impossible for me to be around such a large group anyway because the odds of all twenty-one people being healthy at the same time are probably not in my favor. When I was able to get out of the house but couldn't take the long car ride, I always had friends' homes to go to, and I'm thankful for all the years they included me as family. But now I stay in my air-purified home and am thankful for the opportunity it affords me to breathe easier.

I've never lacked in the food department on the holidays I've spent here alone. I often found it funny that no fewer than three friends, sometimes as many as five, would drop off a plate of food for me so I wasn't missing out on the traditions—which means I probably had enough food in my house to last a week of celebrating! But this year, with my new food allergies, I can't take the risk of eating foods without knowing what's in them and how they're prepared, so I'll be sticking to the items in my own fridge for my Thanksgiving feast.

With one roadblock after another stopping me from the traditions of holidays past, you'd think I'd be really sad about missing out on everything. I sat down to write this, though, after hanging up with a friend who said she was so bummed for me that I would be here alone on the holiday, because I realized that it's really not bothering me very much at all. And I couldn't figure out why.

I mean, of course I'd love to be with all of my family again.

Sure, I'd prefer to get out of the house and socialize with my friends. And yes, diving into mashed potatoes would have been delightful.

It's not that I prefer this. It's that I've learned to appreciate this. I've learned to appreciate the simplicity in my moments. I've learned that being thankful in everything is more important than being thankful for something. I want to be grateful for everything in my life, not just the special moments.

I'm thankful for the years of traditions, and I'm thankful that now I get to reflect on them, remember them, cherish them. I'm thankful to know that my family will be together and my nieces and nephews look forward to seeing each other again. I appreciate hearing my friends' stories about their family get-togethers and the insanity that always ensues. And while I'm not in the middle of all of the festivities, I am still immersed in the blessings of my everyday life.

I am thankful for the system that purifies the air in my condo so I can breathe.

I am thankful for the opportunity to live in the comfort of this condo that is so perfectly suited to me and my needs.

I'm thankful for the program that allows me to hire someone to do my shopping for me and clean my home, so I can live independently.

I'm thankful for my home nurses, who keep tabs on my health so I don't feel overwhelmed by the responsibility.

I'm thankful for the online community that has adopted me into their families, offering more love and support than I knew possible.

I'm thankful for my faith and the peace with which God graces me.

I'm thankful for family and friends who love me, visit me,
call me.

I'm thankful for the abilities I've been able to hold on to, and
I'm thankful I had the chance to experience the abilities
that are no longer mine.

I'm not in the least bit bothered to be here alone on the holiday of gratitude, because it's the same as any other day. I am
simply grateful. I appreciate my life because it's the one He has
given to me, and I don't want to waste a moment of it wishing for
anything else.

୬   ୬   ୬

*Several of the blogs that Sara read participated in something called
Project 365. It was a scrapbooking or photography project in which
people captured a snippet of their lives each day for a year. Friends
urged Sara to participate, since she was an avid photographer and at
one time had been, in her own words, a compulsive scrapbooker. She
was reluctant to join in because she never left her home. How could
she possibly find something new to capture and share each day?*

*Sara decided she was up to the challenge and would get creative—
or, as a last resort, post another picture of Riley. For the last two
years of her life, Sara posted "Gitz Bits" once a week, collections of
one photo per day. And though she did include many pictures of her
photogenic pup, she also gave her readers a peek into her everyday life
and her daily choice to find joy in something new.*

*Joy can certainly be found in a glorious sunset, children running
through a sprinkler, a Caribbean cruise, or mountaintop views. But
Sara refused to miss out on life's joys because she was confined to her
home. She chose to find joy in the small, simple things of life—the
birds visiting the feeder on her porch, an unexpected visitor, a Sonic*

slush delivery from Susie, a win for her favorite football team. She was
grateful for these everyday gifts, she found joy in them, and she praised
God for them.

❦   ❦   ❦

I've been thinking about *praise*, my one word for the year. And what I've come to realize as I've been thinking about praise and how I've focused on it more intentionally is that it all comes down to this: My praise is in direct relation to the thankfulness in my heart. And my thankfulness in all things needs to be in equal measure.

Take, for instance, the day I walked out and saw the "Extreme Home Makeover" some of my family did to my new living space. That was pretty much joy smacking me right in the face and flipping me upside down and backward. Same with people helping me to get a new bed that has made life so much more livable for me. I would have to have been dead not to have my heart beat double time in the happy department.

But just because those things were extraordinary and provided a rush doesn't make them more praiseworthy than the everyday moments of my life.

It's like walking into a restaurant and having dinner with ten of your best friends. Now picture yourself walking into the restaurant and being surprised by those ten friends on your birthday. The first gives you a warm feeling of being surrounded by people you love; the second produces heart-stopping surprise and a rush of joy because of the unexpected. But at the end of the day they are the same friends, and you have the same gratitude for who they are in your life.

I think sometimes we get stuck on the rush. We're stuck needing something to hit us over the head and scream, "Something good just happened!" for us to really stop and take notice. But the reality is that when I stop in my moments and give praise to God, my heart feels the same when I am thanking Him for my room as it does when I'm thanking Him for the sparrow that landed on my feeder.

That's because both are results of His eye being on me as much as it is on that sparrow. God has given me loving and attentive people in my life who provided the bed and the room. He has given me birds that sing to me in the morning and fly around to remind me that life exists beyond these walls. He lets the thunder roll and reminds me of His magnitude. He gives me the ability to walk to the kitchen and reminds me I will always have the strength I need when I need it.

$$9\text{---}9\text{---}9$$

Some of the gifts Sara needed—and received—were people. When her friend Susie's dad died in an accident, Sara was one of the first people to arrive to help Susie's mom, Linda. After that experience, Linda and Sara had a special bond—one that was cemented even further when Linda helped Sara adopt her dog, Riley, by picking him up from a breeder several hours away. Later, when Sara couldn't leave her house at all, Linda delivered her groceries each week and sometimes cooked for her, trying out new recipes they found that would work even with Sara's allergies. When Sara was reluctant to accept the help, Susie explained that her mom truly loved serving Sara, that it made her day to run errands for her or cook her something to eat. The two certainly ended up blessing each other. Sara called Linda her angel, and Linda talked about the joy she received from Sara's friendship: "She was a true inspiration to our whole family, and she changed my life with her faith. I'm so glad to know that someday we'll all be together and will know no pain, only joy!"

$$9\text{---}9\text{---}9$$

Some of God's gifts smack me upside the head and others I need to keep my eyes open to see. But in the end, all are gifts. And all deserve my wholehearted thanks. Every one of them deserves my praise.

Some days are supremely difficult and the pain takes all my energy, while other days His goodness is so obvious. And at the end of both types of days, when I think over the hours and my blessings and I stop to thank Him for all of it, do you know what the difference between them is? Absolutely nothing. Because in the end, love is love. Gift is gift. God is God and He is good. All the time.

And that's why I praise Him through all of it, with the same amount of thanks in my heart. Because, whether obvious or subtle, He is always there with gifts. You just have to be sure you're paying attention.

Sometimes I wonder how changed my vision would be if I had never gotten sick. I have no doubt the core of me would be the same. I would still be compassionate and kind and, some would say, ornery. I know I would have a heart of gratitude, but I'm sure I wouldn't be as aware of the little things.

I want to remember to not just give thanks for the extraordinary moments in my life, the times when I am overwhelmed by grace. I want to be grateful for the ordinary, the basics, the mundane that we assume will always be present. I want to remember to look with eyes that see the ordinary as miracles, so my life can be filled with glory.

9 — 9 — 9

If there's one phrase Sara used most often in her blog, it was "I am so blessed, people." I lost count of the times she began a post giving an update on the latest hard thing in her life, something that had me in tears and would bring the strongest person to her knees, and still wrapped up her thoughts with "I'm so blessed."

My reaction to that kind of gratitude and joy, more often than I'd like to admit, was astonishment. "Who DOES that?" I'd ask my computer screen. Though I was talking to myself each time that happened, I wasn't alone. Family, friends, and blog readers alike found Sara's joy unfathomable at times, and wanted to know how she managed to stay so positive.

❦ ❦ ❦

I realize I talk a lot about being grateful and choosing joy. And we've talked a lot about different ways to keep that focus in our lives. But I don't just plop my feet on the floor every day and see sunshine and rainbows because I've chosen to live a happy life regardless of circumstance. It's not quite that simple—but I realized that in all my talk about this, I have never mentioned the number one thing I do to stay positive, keep my joy, and focus on gratitude. I ask God to help me make the choice.

I seriously about slapped my hand to my forehead and gave myself a V8. I can't believe I forgot to tell you my step one, the step that matters! I want to make sure you all know that before I'm able to make the decision to choose joy, before I am able to look at that Pollyanna silver lining I'm always grasping to see, before I can stop and see the blessing in the midst of the rubble, I am asking Him to open my eyes.

I'm asking Him to change my heart, to change my vision, to create the desire in me to be joyful when I want to close my eyes to all that surrounds me. I close my eyes and open my heart and ask the One Who is the only answer. I ask Him to help me. Today, as my pain was crazy and my soul was tired and the exhaustion clouded my mind, I asked Him to allow me to be the person He made me to be. I asked the One Who gives us everything to help me see everything the way He sees everything.

I also remember that this life is not about me and choose to give thanks to the God Who loves me. That is what keeps my spirits up. It's my focus on praising instead of dwelling on my own circumstances. It's not always easy, but it is something I have to choose to do if I am going to live the life He needs me to.

When things are going smoothly, when things are difficult, when life is in that in between we don't know what to do with, the fact remains that God is good all the time. And that is worth praising Him for. That knowledge, that belief, and that attitude of praise are what shape who we can be in this life for Him.

He knows my past, present, and future. He is surprised by nothing. He is with me, never leaves me even when I feel alone, and holds me up even when I think I am standing on my own two feet. He is good. All the time. I am going to ask Him to help me see that, and I will praise Him through all of it.

9 — 9 — 9

In her book One Thousand Gifts, *Ann Voskamp says, "Prayer without ceasing is only possible in a life of continual thanks." As Sara's faith deepened, what was second nature grew as well. Thanksgiving and gratitude led to praise, which was actually prayer. And Sara spent many of her hours in prayer, praising God and thanking Him for all the many blessings she recognized—including her inability to leave home, because, as she said, "I don't have a lot of distractions between me and God. I don't have a hurried existence. I don't have a job and husband and children and errands or just plain old life to distract me. And in a lot of ways, that really stinks. I would like to have those things filling my world. But in this way, in this I-have-no-one-around-me-but-Jesus way, it has allowed me to have a connection with God I don't know that I could otherwise have. It has*

Sara was one of six stair-step siblings and the baby of her family. From left: Steve (3), Janette (5), Jim (6), Laura (7), Jerry (8).

As the youngest, Sara got to spend lots of time at home with her mom.

Sara's dad taking a minute in his farm office to give Sara a ring for Christmas.

Sara and her mom.

Sara dancing with her dad, the man she adored and called her first boyfriend and her valentine.

Sara and her sisters supporting Mom's dream of opening her own interior design studio. From left: Laura, Sara, Jane, Janette.

Sara with some of her nieces and nephews: Anna, Spencer, Sara, Michael, Becca, Alex, Cooper, Thomas.

Sara, loving life, loving people.

When Sara realized she would never drive her car again, she gave it to her nephew Thomas, who had just turned 16.

Meeting—and holding and playing with and loving on—her friends' kids was one of Sara's biggest joys.

Sara and Mary met in 2009 and had no idea a fun blog connection would turn into a sweet friendship that would turn into a writing partnership.

Mary's daughter, Annalyn, entertained Sara with her vivid imagination during a visit and prayed for Sara every night after meeting her.

Sara's friends Tammy Hodge, Alece Ronzino, and Cathi Stegall had fun eating Oreos in honor of Sara.

Sara documented precious time with her friend Alece Ronzino, even though she was still showing signs of Cushing's disease and was a little camera shy.

Candy Steele, a blog friend who happened to live nearby in Cedar Falls, brought Sara Sonic slushes and fruit almost every week.

Shannon Hayward and her family connected with Sara daily with videos, but visiting and laughing in person was an even bigger gift.

Some of Sara's favorite blog friends Skyping (one of the many ways she maintained friendships online).

Sara considered Jessica Turner family and was thrilled to finally hug her in person in 2011.

Sara was so honored by the gift of writing to Mariela, a young girl in Bolivia sponsored by Matthew and Jessica Turner through World Vision.

Sara's friend Deb taught first and second grade. Her students adopted Sara, sending her notes and cards and videos throughout the year.

The last picture of Sara's entire family together. Back row, from left: Spencer, Jim, Patience, Jerry, Amy, Jeff, Laura, Janette, Steve. Front row, from left: Regan, Amy, Michael, Sara, Alex, Becca, Jane, Mike, Avery (in Mike's lap), Thomas, Anna, Christian (in Anna's lap), and Cooper (front and center).

Sara's ability to create art with words flowered during her illness.

TOO MANY PEOPLE
MISS THE
silver
lining
BECAUSE THEY
ARE EXPECTING
GOLD.

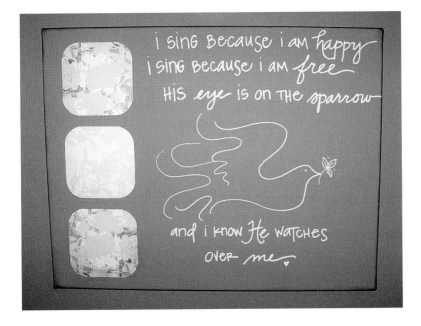

i sing because i am *happy*
i sing because i am *free*
His *eye* is on the *sparrow*

and i know *He* watches
over *me*

no moment from
my God
is a rock of burden.
it's just a rock waiting
to be *broken apart*

✿ ... ✿ ... ✿

into... *stepping stones*

Be 💜
inTenTional
in all things 💜

choose JOY 💜

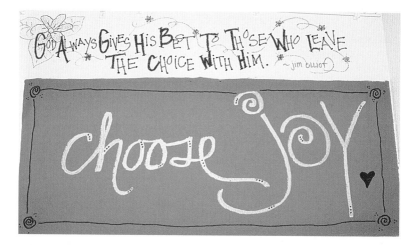

Sara's creativity and love of words and art couldn't be contained. It overflowed into the rooms of her home, like when she grabbed some markers and started coloring on the walls of a converted closet she called her favorite spot in the house.

Be Intentional

Life Goals:

LEADERSHIP IS DOING WHAT IS RIGHT WHEN NO ONE IS WATCHING.

~GEORGE VAN VALKENBERG.

1. To not be ashamed to stand before God.
2. To fulfill God's plan by living the best life I can with what I am given.
3. To be aware and present in every moment.
4. To love what I have, not yearn for what I lack.
5. To spread the Joy, not the fear.
6. To be intentional in all things.

Sara wrote her life goals right on her wall, as a reminder of what was most important to her and what motivated her choices.

Sara's friends Kathy and Kelly spent many evenings snuggled on the couch with Sara (and Riley), eating take-out and watching their favorite TV shows.

Friends Linda and Meg before a birthday dinner at Sara's house. Linda brought groceries to Sara once a week, often cooking for Sara or even bringing along her grandsons (and Sara's godsons), Jonathan and Tyler.

Sara and her faith sharing group met every other week. From top left, clockwise: Meg, Susie, Leslie, Deb.

Meg, Susie, and their kids wished Sara a merry Christmas from the safety of her patio. They couldn't come in without spreading germs but made sure Sara felt loved on the holidays.

The (in)courage writers Skyping with Sara, pictured from top left: Kristen Strong, Holley Gerth, Lainie Button, Lysa TerKeurst, Stephanie Bryant, Ann Voskamp, Deidra Riggs, Robin Dance, Lisa-Jo (and Zoe) Baker, Lisa Leonard, Bonnie Gray, Jessica (and Adeline) Turner, Sarah Markley, Emily Freeman.

Sara had the chance to Skype with the (in)courage writers during their annual beach retreat, shortly before she passed away.

Riley took his job as "blog dog" seriously and insisted on being photographed and featured regularly.

Though Sara resisted buying and using a walker initially, "George" (as she named it) quickly became convenient and then necessary to Sara's comfort and mobility in her home.

With her family during her last days. From left: Jerry, Mom, Sara, Laura, Janette, Steve, Jim.

During her last days Sara gathered her friends to speak with them and love them one last time. From left: Jenny, Nicole, Sara, Katie, Meg.

Sara with her nurse and friend Tabetha.

Sara with her friend Susie during her last days.

Receiving last rites from her priest.

After Sara's passing,
many people got tattoos
in her honor.

A note from Sara's
dad that she had
framed.

Love you –
will be talking
to you soon

Love Dad

become as natural for me to connect with Him as it is for me to blink my eyes."

ᴕ   ᴕ   ᴕ

As I was talking about prayer with Susie the other day, I told her that at some point my prayer life had changed. Now every one starts with, "Thank You."

I don't know how else to pray because I stopped knowing what I wanted to pray for. As much as I want parts of my life to change, I don't want them to change if it's not in the best plan of God. Sometimes I don't want things to be this hard if I live a long life, and sometimes I want to fulfill this road but want Him to promise me it will be a short one. I want my friends and family protected and to feel the peace they so need, but I don't want them to be protected out of living and loving in His will.

For me, it all comes down to wanting to ask Him for His will to be done. Not mine. It comes down to trusting Him with absolutely everything and everyone. So my prayers sound more like this:

- Thank You for knowing how all of this plays out each day, so I can be content in living each day of it for You.
- Thank You for keeping me open so I can see what is in front of me that You need from me today.
- Thank You for covering my friend in Your protection. For allowing her to feel the love and peace that I am sending and that You provide.
- Thank You for never leaving my friend, even when he doesn't feel You or believe in You; thank You for waiting for him with open arms when he's ready to see You again.
- Thank You for loving her enough to make a clear path in a time when she needs to know how to travel.

- Thank You for the gifts You've placed everywhere around me, in the hard places, so I can see You in them all more clearly.
- Thank You for healing her in Your time and in the way You know she needs. For protecting her body and her spirit as only You know how to do as she walks this road.

I don't know if I'm right or wrong, but I trust that everything that comes from God is good. I trust that everything that comes from God is an already-answered prayer. I trust that everything that will come from God is exactly what I need. Even if it's hard. Because He sees what I can't. So I count it all as gift. And I thank Him—not for the pain and the difficulty—but for the faithfulness He gives during all of it.

That is how I have learned how to praise. Even in my weakest places, even in my hardest moments, even in the depths of pain and sickness, I thank Him for what I know for sure is true—beyond the distraction of the hard, within the hard.

I praise Him for Him. As Ann says in her book, all is gift. All is grace. And I praise Him because I trust Him with all of it. My praise and my trust go hand in hand.

> ✎ — ✎ — ✎

Sara was an inspiration to everyone who knew her and even to many who never met her. Family, friends, and blog readers said often how her life encouraged them to live differently, to choose joy in their own lives. But those same friends and family knew how much Sara hated to worry or bother them, so occasionally they'd check in to make sure that when she said, "It's all good" that it really was all good. Sara was honest about her struggles and never wanted to paint a pretty—but inaccurate—picture of her life for people. But even when prompted to share more of the gritty reality of her life, she still ended up focusing on the positive.

Sara wrote a post for her friend Tam's blog, but insisted that Tam choose the topic. That is how she ended up writing a post called "Confessions of a Homebound Girl: The Ugly Truth," a title Sara said sounded as if it should be followed by an ominous "dun, dun, dun"! As you'll see, even when prompted to write about the ugly parts of life, Sara still pointed us to the beauty.

9 — 9 — 9

I'm not a girl who usually looks at my life as having an ugly truth. But the more I thought about it, the more I realized that the ugly truth is this: life isn't fair. And balance has nothing to do with things being equal.

Life isn't fair. But it wasn't meant to be.

What we tend to forget is that we created the idea of fair. God didn't. He never told us we deserve a perfect existence. He never told us life would be simple if we were faithful. He just told us to be faithful, and that He would be, too. I embraced that concept and realized that as long as I stay focused on Him and what He needs from me, rather than what I want for me, my life will be full and balanced. Not fair. Not good and bad in what I consider equal measure. But balanced with His mercy—an ugly truth partnered with a beautiful one.

The ugly truth is that I wake up in the morning, after a fitful night of sleep, with more pain than my brain can register. I wake up, take my meds, and spend about an hour trying to figure out the best way to get out of bed that day.

The beautiful truth is that I have this little white pup who lies with me regardless of how long it takes. He's like my own physical therapy as I pet him and try to get my fingers and arms moving. If I close my eyes again, he snuggles with me, and if I open them he plays hide-and-seek with the covers to keep me entertained until I can sit up and start moving.

The ugly truth is that it became dangerous for me to do something as simple as shower because stepping into the tub was a major feat. Taking a bath, while therapeutic, was impossible because I couldn't get down into the tub, and if I had I certainly would never have been able to get back up.

The beautiful truth is that my Ill and Handicapped Waiver provided me with a walk-in bathtub, ensuring my safety and comfort and, more importantly, ensuring my independence.

The ugly truth is that I spend at least 95 percent of my life in seclusion. I can only let perfectly healthy people into my condo. If you come in with an ear infection, I could wind up with pneumonia. The ugly truth is that while my life came to a standstill, everyone else's lives continued to get busier, which means I can go long periods of time alone. I sometimes go many months not seeing anyone but my home nurses, Dawn (who cleans my home every other week), and Linda (who delivers my groceries). And sometimes I don't even see them if they are sick or have been around sick people.

The beautiful truth is that I still feel connected. My friends call, they Skype, they videotape their kids' school concerts I'm missing, they tell me in detail about the events I miss and the daily happenings I so want to be a part of.

The ugly truth is that I don't care about what I can't do for myself; I care about what I can't do for others. I care about not being there for my nieces and nephews, their future graduations and weddings and joys and sorrows. I care about not being there for people I love when someone dies, when they need consoling and my arms can't be wrapped around them. The ugly truth is that I'm fine with what I have lost; I'm not fine with what I can no longer give.

The beautiful truth is that I was able to spend many years establishing relationships that last beyond physical boundaries.

The beautiful truth is that, while I can't leave my home to be with them, I am always home to take their calls. I get to be their refuge away from their realities. The beautiful truth is that I still get to serve them; I just serve them differently.

The ugly truth is that I had to let go of my dream of writing to make a living, but once I started blogging I realized I was writing to make a life. To meet new people. To open up my world. To fill my life with authentic relationships I would never have been exposed to had I been given the chance to live the busy life I always dreamed of having.

The beautiful truth is that being homebound isn't limiting my life. It's just limiting my location.

※　　※　　※

The ugliest truth of the last couple of years of Sara's life is that her dad passed away and she was unable to attend his funeral or grieve beside her family. Because it hurt physically to cry, she wasn't even able to grieve the way she wanted. It was a dark time as Sara tried to make sense of what had happened and what it meant for her family, her life, her faith. In the end, just as she did during every other challenge life handed her, Sara chose to cling to her faith, believing that God was just as good now as He had been before her dad's death. She chose to continue seeking joy, to continue thanking God, to continue praising His name.

※　　※　　※

I am so grateful.

That's what I've been thinking about tonight as I lie here with my thoughts, resting and thinking about family gathering together at my parents' house to remember all that happened a year ago. As I think about losing my dad, as I think about not being with my family, as I think about my own life and what's ahead. As I try to peer into the unknown future to catch a glimpse of what I'm supposed to do and who I'm supposed to be.

In all of that, through all of that, every time I open my lips to speak to Him I can only speak of how grateful I am.

> I am so grateful I had the dad I did. I'm so grateful that I was a young girl who grew up to know she was loved by her dad and never had to search for that love in anyone who didn't value her.
>
> I am so grateful I had a dad who brought laughter into every single day and brought tenderness into every single hurt. I am so grateful I had a dad who taught me faith by his example and taught me trust by the steps he took.
>
> I am so grateful that my family is together to honor him and am so grateful that he will be remembered in their laughter and their tears and their memories.
>
> I am so grateful that I know God well enough that I can trust His design for me even in a future that is beyond my sight, and I am so grateful that the same God knows me well enough to always provide exactly what I need exactly when I need it.
>
> I am grateful for the blessings that always come out of pain. I am grateful for the people and the friendships and the soul-embracing moments that can only come from shared experience.

I have been given so much and I have treasured so much and I have lost so much. And I am so grateful.

9

Giving What We Are

On Serving and Community

We must not only give what we have; we must give
what we are.   —Cardinal Désiré-Joseph Mercier

*Sara struggled with both sides of serving—feeling unable to serve
others, as well as having to allow others to serve her. But at the end
of the day, she always came back to the conclusion that her life was
not about her; it was about what God wanted to do with it and whom
He wanted to touch through her. It's no wonder, then, that regardless
of her physical limitations Sara insisted on seeking community and
relationships and ways to help people. Just as God redefined every
other part of her life, He changed the way Sara connected with
people, too.*

*After she passed away, Sara's friends and family shared story
after story about her. As the memories and anecdotes wove a
rich tapestry of Sara's life, a common thread throughout was her
commitment to serving others, her giving spirit. Some of the stories
were heartbreakingly beautiful, like the one about how she supported*

her friend Kelly when Kelly's eleven-year-old daughter Kaitlyn died of cancer, and how she devoted herself to praying for other friends who'd lost loved ones. Some were funny, like the one about Meg calling her one night in a fit over her husband's forgetting to pick up a potato at the store for the school project of one of their kids. Now, Meg said, she just has to say the word potato *to her husband and they both crack up. Whether it was a friend calling to report a devastating car accident or another calling in the midst of postpartum depression and newborn fatigue, Sara's response was, "I'll be right there." And she truly was there for her friends and family, even when she was confined physically, giving to them everything she possibly could every time.*

ꝯ — ꝯ — ꝯ

It's not about me.

That's what has been popping into my head a lot lately when people ask me questions about how I deal with being sick, why I don't get more frustrated, why I don't complain more, or why I'm not angry about my situation.

We all want life to be fair. We want goodness to prevail and hard work to mean that life will be easier. And that green grass on the other side of the fence that belongs to the people who don't appreciate it? We'd like that to be transplanted into the lawn of the person who spends all day feeding and watering their sparse-looking grass in hopes of a fruitful harvest.

But all of that is "me" thinking—and it's not about me.

The plain and simple truth, if we take big lessons in life and strip them down to the bare essentials, is that we are tiny blips on a very big screen. Only God has the capacity to see all of it. He saw all that came before us and sees all that will come after us, and only He can know the role that each of us can play that will best serve Him and each other.

So my life isn't ideal by our standards. By my standards it's getting less ideal by the year. That whole living-in-pain thing? I could do without it. The getting-sick thing? Gets old really fast. The never-leaving-the-house thing? I could think of some fun places to go. I miss fresh air. I miss singing at church. I miss dancing until I'm out of breath and riding in a boat so fast you feel like you're flying if you close your eyes.

But it's not about me. It's about what He can do with my life. I have learned a lot about myself, my faith, my perspective. But that doesn't mean I was given this illness to teach me something. For all I know, God saw this illness was going to be in my body and helped nurture me so I could use it to affect someone else. And as much as I would like this disease to be gone when I wake up in the morning, if it serves to make another person see their life or relationship with God in a new light, then I wouldn't ask for it to be taken from me.

Because it's not about me. Nothing about my life is about me; it's about whom He needs me to be. And how can I complain about that?

Oh, complaining can come so easily for all of us: your small house, your flat tire, the promotion that should have been yours and the grass that grows so fast you don't have the time to mow it . . .

But what if the small house is so you are next to a neighbor who needs your help when her husband dies? Or your tire went flat when you were driving so it didn't happen when your teenage son was driving and he wouldn't have known what to do? Maybe the promotion would have been a dead end for you and next year a better opportunity will be waiting. And that lawn? Maybe it's the only exercise you do each week and is saving you from a heart attack.

The point is that you don't know. I don't know. But it's not about me. It's about how He can use my life. So as far as I'm concerned, even those things that make me want to pull my hair out and scream, "Why me?!?" are blessings in disguise. Blessings for me, or for someone else, or for a reason I can't even imagine. But it doesn't really matter. Because it's not about me.

❧ ❧ ❧

If anyone could have let herself off the hook for not serving others, it was Sara. If anyone had a valid excuse for focusing on herself, it was Sara. But she wasn't having any of that. She refused to be reduced by her circumstances, to let her limitations keep her from fulfilling God's plan for her. Her friend Candy called her a "chronic giver" who loved immensely, no matter what. Sara's friend Tam wrote about her giving spirit as well, saying, "Sara had an amazing selflessness about her. In a world where our culture is so self-focused and entitled, she had every right to play that card. More than anyone else I know. But she didn't—not once. Her medication was to pour into others. That was balm for her soul. Every day, when she was well and strong enough, I got a text or call from her asking about the family. She loved our kids so much! And it wasn't an escape for her; it was an act of obedience and faith to give to others as long as she had breath to do so."

❧ ❧ ❧

Things have changed quite a bit for me in the last year. (Feel free to call me Captain Obvious.) Losing abilities is nothing new to me; I've sat by and watched parts of my life and talents slip away for the last fifteen years. Some of them faded gradually; others left in the blink of an eye, never to return.

I had become accustomed to walking more slowly, pacing

myself with activities around the house, limiting any repetitive movements, and accepting the flow of my body on any given day. But then I spent many months completely immobile this past year. And like a wave that crashes on the beach and throws the sand out into the abyss of the ocean, that immobility hit me hard. The changes I had become accustomed to were flung out into that vast unknown. So I'm relearning my new normal, but I never want my physical limits to change who I strive to be.

I've accepted that my mobility is more limited, my stamina and energy are decreased, my feet are more tender, and my hands are less useful. But what I've noticed lately is that, while my life and mobility stopped this summer, my sense of time stopped as well.

Months seem to run together. Days absolutely run together. I have no idea when I wake in the morning if it's the beginning of the week or the end of it until I look at my pill dispenser and realize what day I'm on. And that's okay. I'm no longer as concerned with what is supposed to happen each day as I'm concerned with being open to the day. Being open to accomplishing what I can when I'm able, being open to resting when my body demands it, being open to remaining present in my moments so I can take advantage of whatever is in front of me.

But just because my hands and feet no longer serve me well physically, I don't want that to be an excuse to not be the hands and feet of God.

Along with losing track of the days, I've also lost track of important dates. Important birthdays have gone by unnoticed and unacknowledged. I have so many thank-you notes left unwritten that I'm not sure whom I've sent them to and who has been neglected. Little people who always receive valentines from me didn't this year because I forgot the day existed until I got something in the mail.

I know I have an excuse. My pain and exhaustion have my brain flying at half-mast on a good day. There are many things I have let go of out of necessity, but if there is one thing I should hold on to for dear life, it's my focus on others.

For Lent this year, every time I try to use my hands and they fail me, every time I walk on my feet and feel the deep ache it causes, it's going to be my reminder that while my physical hands and feet are weak, they are not limiting me from being the hands and feet of Christ.

I know I'm not able to do grand things for great numbers of people, but I am going to consciously choose to stay focused on others, to be His hands and feet in the little ways that matter to people. I'm going to remember why I am here, even if I'm not sure what day it is.

9 — 9 — 9

Sara made a regular practice of turning my understanding of spiritual matters upside down—and how I viewed those in need was no different. Always striving to be more of the person God intended her to be, a better version of herself that shone the light of God, Sara wasn't content to stop at simply feeling grateful for her blessings. When confronted with the incredible needs of others—especially those suffering from poverty or the aftermath of natural disasters—Sara thanked God for providing for her needs but quickly moved on to ask how she could help.

9 — 9 — 9

We've all been there, right? We have a needy child or spouse (well, I don't, but you might), or a needy boss or neighbor (okay, I might be the needy neighbor). We feel needy when we think we're neglected. We need new technology, just the right outfit, a long-overdue manicure, the bigger house that suits our idea of success. We are needy, needy people.

Except we're not. Even in this economy, most people reading this have a roof over their head, food in their fridge, and clothes on their backs. At the very least, you're in a place that has a computer and Internet access. Which means we are spoiled rotten rich.

"The poor aren't on earth for us to think, 'Phew, how blessed am I that it's not me.'" When I saw someone post that statement on Twitter, it hit me in the gut. I am the first to tell you I realize how blessed I am. I have everything I could possibly need and then some, despite my health and disability status. There are so many who struggle more than me.

Phew, how blessed am I that it's not me.

Ugh. Instead of making that statement, I should be asking a question: What am I doing about all those who aren't me? Those who don't have family and friends and disability payments? It's not enough to be grateful and go about my business.

⟿ ⟿ ⟿

It wasn't lip service on Sara's part when she talked about helping those in need. Her disease kept her from leaving her home to serve, and her tight budget kept her from giving lavishly. But Sara was creative in more ways than one, and she sought ways to serve just as she sought community.

Through blogging and social media, Sara made dozens of close friends who lived all around the world. Some of them grew to be as close as family—and some even were able to visit Sara in person. In a beautiful marriage of service and community, two of Sara's closest friends—Matthew and Jessica Turner—gave her the precious gift of a child sponsorship through World Vision. Then, while Matthew was visiting Sara's sponsored child in Bolivia, Jessica and their kids came to visit Sara in her home. The joy Sara felt about both parts of this were almost tangible through the screen.

⸙ ⸙ ⸙

When I got to know Jessica and Matthew, these beautiful people came to me, opened their hearts, and let me be a part of their family. We call, we Skype, we text. We share our good times and our rough times. They've seen me on camera without makeup and barely talking, and they love me as if I'm peppy and easily heard.

They love the way I love. With everything they are. And when you're hit with that kind of acceptance you are never the same. I'm not the same.

On Monday, Jessica walked right through my door and hugged me, and it felt to me like she'd just finally come home. I don't know how else to explain it.

While Jess was here showing off her babes to me, Matthew was in Bolivia for World Vision. And a few months ago, around my birthday, he and Jess called to tell me they wanted to do something special. They wanted to let me choose a child to sponsor in the village Matthew was going to visit.

And my heart chose Mariela. This beautiful ten-year-old girl, who comes from a big family with two brothers and six sisters, is now going to be helped because of Matthew and Jessica's choice to sponsor her with World Vision. This sponsorship will help provide Mariela and her community with school supplies and new classrooms, as well as clean water and ongoing medical care, and improved nutrition and hygiene. Her mom will learn job skills that will help them increase their family income and raise their standard of living, and through Christian witness she will have a chance to know the love and grace of God.

And she's going to know she is loved and cared for, by God and by me, because I'm going to write to her and remind her all the time.

You can't have too much family to love.

9 — 9 — 9

When I search the archives of my e-mail for conversations I had with Sara, the note that makes me smile biggest is just one sentence long. One Christmas eve she e-mailed me and asked how my church solo had gone. Now, that might not seem unusual, but I was so pleasantly surprised to read that message. The Internet is a big place, a busy place full of people and posts and messages and ministries and opinions and opportunities. Even for someone with as much time on her hands as Sara, the Web holds infinite possibilities for entertainment and time spent. I'd mentioned in passing days earlier that I was nervous about singing a solo at church and, though I counted Sara as a friend and knew she cared about our conversations, I expected my concern to be lost in cyberspace as quickly as a tweet or Facebook update.

I should have known better. Sara wasn't like "normal" friends who have great intentions but forget to reply, or totally care a lot about whatever's going on in your life but never bother to follow up with you. Not Sara. Sara followed up, Sara asked and prayed and cared and remembered. I think a lot of that was due to her devotion to paying attention, to listening, to being fully present with whoever was in front of her—whether in person, on the phone, or through the computer screen. Her friend Amie said, "A minute-long conversation with Sara and you felt like you were the only person in the world."

This was a theme I heard over and over from Sara's friends and family. If Sara was with you, she was WITH you. Whether she was snuggled on her couch with friends Kathy and Kelly enjoying a Mike's Hard Lemonade and takeout from Applebee's, Skyping and laughing

with Ellyn, Amie, and Mandy about everything from spiritual matters
to the best jeans for their bodies, opening up all her paint to decorate
canvases with her friend Shannon's little girls, or fulfilling her fairy
godmother duties by watching a Hot Wheels Battle Force 5 *marathon*
with Susie's son Jonathan, Sara savored each moment with the people
she loved and made each one feel like the most important person in
that moment.

୭ ୭ ୭

I used to be a major multitasker. In my "before" life I would
have been watching TV, talking on the phone, and writing
a blog post all at the same time. I rarely read a book without
also listening to music. In college, I didn't enjoy studying at the
library. I'd rather go to the student union and let the murmur of
activity and people lull me into focus on my studies or twenty-
page papers.

I grew up in a house with five siblings. Noise was the background of my world. But that's not who I am anymore. In this
"after" life, I crave silence. And I do not multitask. Ever. If I am
responding to an e-mail, the music gets turned off. If I am reading through tweets or blogs, the television is turned to mute.
If we are talking on the phone, you can be assured I am doing
nothing but listening to the sound of your voice. Whatever is in
front of me gets my full attention. And I like it better this way.

Just because we aren't face-to-face doesn't mean your words
on the screen are any less important to me. Just because a friend
can't sit in my living room doesn't mean they don't need my
undivided attention. Life, I have learned, is meant to be savored.
And we are missing so much of it.

Be honest. How many times have you been on the phone,
folding laundry, keeping an eye on your kid while halfheartedly
paying attention to the movie they are watching on TV, only to

realize you have no idea what the person on the other end of the phone has said for the last three minutes?

I'm not criticizing. I know we live in a world where life doesn't get done unless we do it all at the same time. It's just that my life changed for me, and that's when I realized all I was missing. I don't multitask now because the pain is relentless and my focus isn't what it used to be. I don't sleep much anymore and the exhaustion has fried my brain. (We won't even talk about the twenty-three different medications I take. I am your brain on drugs. Any questions?)

I have to focus. Life made me focus. And I realize now I should have spent more time focusing as a choice instead of what it is now: a necessity.

This focus makes a difference in my prayer life, too. I've learned that when I read my Bible, talk to God for a few minutes, and then turn on the TV right away, I've appeased God instead of acknowledging Him. I've put in some time and then gone about my business, assuming the rest will take care of itself. But if I'm always busy, always surrounded with noise, always occupied, I will never hear Him. I will never listen.

Sometimes the pain and activity of my body is so loudly incessant that I crave the quiet just to balance my existence. But it has been in those silent times, when my mind drifts into thoughts and topics at random, that I get sparks of Him. I get an idea or a conclusion or a peace that I know has nothing to do with me. But I have to be quiet. I have to be with Him.

❧   ❧   ❧

When asked what brought her the most joy, Sara always replied without hesitation that her nieces and nephews did that. She adored those kids with every fiber of her being and showed them every chance she got. When they were younger and she was less sick and more

active, Sara loved attending their every game, recital, and picnic in
the park. But as she became unable to leave her house, her time with
those she loved most was restricted along with her mobility. When
she missed her oldest nephew's graduation, it took her a bit to work
through her disappointment, but eventually she remembered that even
though she wouldn't show up in any of the graduation party photos,
she had been there in spirit and they had been with her.

﹖﹖﹖

In May of this year, my oldest nephew graduated from high
school. It was one of those moments when I realized why all of
my family still thinks of me as a twelve-year-old—because sometimes, no matter how much we grow up, people freeze in time in
our minds. My nephew is still stuck in my memories as a little
dude who would sing "Blue Suede Shoes" with me and make me
read *If You Give a Mouse a Cookie* at least fifteen times in a row.

Even at eighteen, when I ask him if he knows how much I love
him, he'll respond with, "Around the world and back, Aunt Sara."
And he says it with the same certainty as when he was three.
Knowing how I love him, you can imagine how much I wanted
to be there to celebrate his accomplishment. But I couldn't be. I
was here. As always.

There was a community of people around him, but I wasn't
one of them.

When my family was taking photos at his party, my mom and
sisters posed for a photo, but it was hard for them to do. My
sister Laura wasn't sure they should. My mom said it just didn't
feel right to have one missing. My sister Janette, who has way
too much confidence in me, convinced them both that I could
Photoshop myself into the picture so it would seem like I had
been there.

I, of course, couldn't. But I also didn't think I should. I think there comes a time when we need to make sure we aren't longing instead of living.

The truth is, I wasn't there. Photoshopping myself into the photo wouldn't have been reality. And the reality is, even though I wasn't physically there, physically in the photo, that doesn't mean I'm not still a part of their community.

When I think of community, I think of Matthew 18:20, when Jesus said, "For where two or three have gathered together in My name, I am there in their midst." To me, the part that stands out is that they are gathered in His name. The people I love, the people who are in the community of my heart, are those who are gathered with God in their hearts. Because we all share that common bond of love and belief, we are all tied together—whether we are physically together or not.

I thought of that as I looked at the photo of my beautiful mom and sisters—and they are my community. I think of it as friends online, whom I will most likely never meet, share their lives and hearts with me—and they are my community. I think of it as friends take me along in their everyday lives with video or take photos during their vacations just so I can get a glimpse of what they see—and they are my community.

I thought of it when I was once again separate from my family as they gathered for my dad's funeral, as I watched and loved them all from my computer screen here in my condo. I am always going to be physically separated from the rest of the world. I am always going to be isolated and homebound here in my condo.

But I don't have to be without community. I don't have to choose longing instead of living. Because we are gathered in His name, because we love and believe with hearts that love God more than ourselves, we are a community. A living, breathing community that has learned how to share our lives over any distance.

Jesus told us to do this life together, as a community. And because of Him, there are no boundaries. There is only the common bond of belief and love.

9 — 9 — 9

When Sara invested so deeply in relationships with her family and friends before getting sick, she had no idea how much she would need those relationships later in life. She wasn't laying foundations in order to lean on them when life got hard and connecting grew difficult. She was simply loving her people. But God knew. God knew how rough Sara's road would be and how badly she would need community. She listened when He prompted her to nurture her relationships—and when He planted the seed for a blog that might reach kindred spirits she wouldn't have met otherwise. And when she needed support most, all those people were there, ready to love her and hold her up.

Sara's mom said that when Sara first started her blog, her family was nervous but quickly realized its benefit. It changed Sara's life; as her sister Laura said, social media was Sara's lifesaver. Toward the end of her life, Sara's friend Matthew wrote about the difference social media had made to her, saying, "For three years, Sara's window to the outside world has been a computer screen and an iPad. From the confines of a nine-hundred-square-foot apartment in Iowa, she reached out into the blogosphere and found people to love, to cry with, to share joy with, to experience life with. Those small windows not only gave her a view of the outside world, they opened up and let the outside world in so we could share, love, cry, and experience life with Sara.

"We've shared birthdays with Sara. Christmases with Sara. Vacations with Sara. Our joys and successes with Sara. And our broken moments with Sara. Social media allowed us to do that.

We complain about social media a lot. But for Sara, it is a lifeline,
perhaps God's hands, albeit his digital hands, reaching out to her."

๑ — ๑ — ๑

My year of being thirty-six was, by far, the most difficult year
I've faced yet. It was definitely the most painful. And it was,
hands down, the most exhausting. Thirty-six was also one of the
most beautiful years I've lived through. It was one of the most
grace-filled, and was abundant in blessings. I didn't know it
would be so difficult. But I also had no idea how blessed this year
would be.

> I didn't know that all of you would step up and be a lifeline
> of support for me when I could barely raise my head off
> the pillow.
> I didn't know that some of my family would drop things in
> their lives to hunt down doctors in their offices for me,
> or that friends would show up with new clothes to try to
> make me feel better about not fitting into anything I used
> to wear, and different gadgets to make my space functional.
> I didn't know that I would form new bonds with people
> through the vast cyberspace—and I certainly didn't know
> that some of those Internet friends would be walking into
> my home and hugging me around the neck.
> I didn't know that random kindness would show up at my
> door in the form of cards and notes of love that filled
> me up and kept me focused. I didn't know that I would
> find even more friends who would become family to me.
> I didn't know the community of people on blogs and
> Twitter would rally to love me in the darkest places
> where pain would leave me secluded and alone.

I didn't know. But I should have known. Because some form of all of these "I didn't know"s happen to each of us every year. And I've never gone through one of those years without everything I needed, because He provides me with what I need, when I need it.

ƎƎƎ

Something God gave Sara when she needed it was a new friend. Candy was someone she met through blogging who ended up living in her town! After seeing Candy mention her town in a comment on another blog, Sara eventually learned that they lived just seven miles apart and shared several friends. Of course they had to meet—and Candy was able to serve Sara right from the beginning. "Yep, I totally made her do me a favor the first time we were meeting in person. Yep, that really drove me nuts. I kind of thought I'd have her over for dinner or something before I started bossing her around, but I guess she's initiated now."

Candy was happy to help but got her back for that "favor" by trying to convince Sara to eat healthier. She wrote on her blog, "We quickly realized we had a lot of mutual acquaintances, we lived just a few miles apart, and we shared a love for food. Well, we don't love the same food, but We. Love. Food. I tried to convince her to eat mine ('Sara, this açai juice will go right to your cells!') and she extolled the qualities of bacon. Our common food ground is fruit. She loves fresh fruit, and it tickled me to no end the first time I brought her a pomegranate. I mean, they had poms in the Bible, right? 'Where have these been?? Are they NEW??' 'I'm pretty sure Jesus ate pomegranates, Sara. They may have even been put on the ark. Just savor the explosion in your mouth.' 'NO, I just want to EAT them!!' Funny girl, that one."

Never did Sara take for granted the uncommon friendships and fiercely devoted family she had. She recognized them as her biggest blessings and never missed an opportunity to express her love and gratitude.

~ ~ ~

I'm thankful for those I love who are near. My friends who call on their way home from work, who drop me off a Sonic slush for no reason other than that they know it makes me smile, who would walk through my door if their health let them, and who would stand outside my window just to wave if they thought I needed to see a friendly face.

I am so very blessed.

I'm thankful for those I love who are far. My friends and family who call when I've been quiet, who text and e-mail and Skype to keep me a part of their lives. For those who send me pictures of sunsets and videos while on walks or while simply sitting at their desks at work—just to give me a glimpse of the world outside my walls. They love me as I am, where I am.

I am so very blessed.

I'm thankful for my pesky pup. The one who lies with me for hours on end and would rather snuggle under covers than retrieve a ball or romp outside. I'm also thankful he pesters me now and then for fresh water and makes me get up out of bed even when it hurts, because I count him as my physical therapist for pushing me beyond my comfort. And I count him as my counselor, too, as he lets me cry and makes me laugh and keeps me sane.

I am so very blessed.

I'm thankful for my faith. I'm thankful for the deepest knowledge that there is a God and He loves me. I am so very grateful that He came to earth and saved the world so we can all be together someday for eternity. Without knowing that, I couldn't do what He needs of me in the here and now.

I am so very blessed.

I'm so very thankful for all of my blog friends. Friends and readers who are the dessert at the end of a very filling meal. Those who show up here, who found me sitting by myself on the other end of this computer screen and decided to stick around and keep me company. Those who remind me, every single day, that I am not doing this life alone.

I am so very blessed.

10

God's Best

On Being Thankful for What You Had

God always gives His best to those who leave the choice with Him.

—Jim Elliot

Sara didn't gloss over the loss in her life. She mourned the husband, the children, the career, and the many experiences she would never have. But she never stayed in her grief long before remembering that even though her life was not what she'd dreamed of or planned, it was still a life full of amazing blessings. When reflecting on a letter she'd written to her future self about what her life would look like, she joked about how consistently wrong she had been about every part of her imagined future. But she also wrote about how thankful she was for the life she'd lived, despite the long list of things she'd never be able to do. More importantly, Sara loved the life she'd been given and the people who filled it. From her parents to her friends to her beloved nieces and nephews, she adored them and soaked up every moment she had with them.

I opened my mail one day this week and had an envelope from my friend Nicole. Inside was a sheet of paper that said, "5 Years from Now..." I had forgotten it, but at Nicole's bachelorette party we all wrote down where we thought we'd be in five years. I assume we were supposed to get it back before now, as they've been married eight years, but since she has two girls and is pregnant with twins, we'll give her a break. My old predictions were pretty entertaining:

> I'd love to be married with a child, maybe through adoption. I will have at least one of my children's books published and will be working on a book of short stories. I will have made another recording for my family and friends of different songs and will sing at a jazz club at least once— just to say that I did. I will have vacationed in New York and gone to see a couple of Broadway musicals. My future husband will, of course, take me to New York often just so I can get my fix of culture.

Well, fortune-teller I am not. It would have been encouraging if at least one of these predictions had come true, but maybe I get points for getting them all wrong? Kind of like when you play the card game hearts and try taking all the hearts for higher points rather than getting rid of them?

I have to admit that when I opened the envelope and realized what it contained, I was hesitant to read the letter. I couldn't remember what I had written and didn't know if I wanted to stir up painful emotions. So as I read through the predictions and nodded my head, remembering how sure I had been of them, I took a deep breath and waited for it to happen.

I waited for the sadness. I waited for the longing. I waited to be wistful. I waited for the envy to creep in for that girl who had existed. I waited. And nothing.

It's not that I felt nothing; I wasn't unaffected. But I was unburdened in a way. It was simply a memory of another time. I thought of how lovely it is that I was able to have those dreams. I had the chance once upon a time to think those things were possible. I had such fun that summer celebrating with Nicole and having that time in my life when it seemed like everything was within my grasp. It's not sad those things didn't come true; it's a joy that I had the chance to dream about the future.

When you're younger, you want to get older so badly, because you think you'll be settled. You'll finally have the job and the house and the husband and the kids. You assume that as life goes on things will become clearer and you'll be more settled and everything will fall into place.

And then life happens. You shake your head and laugh at the younger version of yourself for believing life would turn out just as you imagined it. And you look back on the road you've traveled and marvel at how, at every turn, you were upheld and loved. You were provided for. You were sustained through every change and every challenge.

My reaction to that letter surprised me (which makes sense, as apparently I'm not that great at predictions), but I'm not sure it's how I would have reacted had I not been writing on my blog. I started this simply for something to do. My convictions and beliefs and outlook on life haven't changed. But I do think saying what you believe out loud (or in writing) makes it so much easier to live your convictions. The fact that I have been writing about how grateful I am for the blessings in my life made it easier to read that letter. It made it possible to appreciate the dreams of that twenty-seven-year-old version of myself, while still being a happy thirty-five-year-old living a totally different reality.

I learned this over and over as I got sicker and lost so many abilities. I remember thinking that it made absolutely no sense to me that God would give me so many talents and gifts, and then not let me have the opportunity to keep using them. So many things I loved to do were slowly being stripped away, and because I had used them for His glory I couldn't understand how being without them could be the right thing.

He gave me a voice to sing His praises, and I used it to lead worship at church, sing at wedding celebrations, and bring peace to those at funerals. I spoke at and led retreats, I was social and did good deeds for others when I was out and about in the world. I lived life happy, dancing and laughing and trying to bring joy to people. I couldn't understand why He had given me the gifts if they were just going to be taken away.

But then I learned that I'd had the gifts when He needed me to use them. I didn't squander and waste my talents, and they brought Him glory when they were supposed to. And I realized that if my talents were gone, if they were taken from me, then it was because I wasn't supposed to have them anymore.

I trusted that He saw the bigger picture, and I stepped forward in faith by living the life that was in front of me. I stepped forward, knowing that whatever He wanted from me now, He would make sure I had the gifts to use in the moment. My gifts back then served God's purpose, and if they were gone, so was that purpose.

9　9　9

More than any other gifts, Sara was thankful for her family and her friends—and the time she had to invest in them before her life was so limited. After she'd been sharing stories about her family for a while, she admitted that she'd received more than one e-mail asking how she could possibly not have any unpleasant childhood memories. She responded with humor and honesty: "Are you freaking kidding me? Life is not all sunshine and roses. We are human, people. But it's all good."

She refused to write anything that could hurt the people she loved, but when she looked at her life and her family, Sara really did believe it was all good. From the Friday nights she spent during her childhood dancing to Lawrence Welk with her five stair-step siblings to the family dinners she spent at the kids' table with her nieces and nephews long after she was an adult (but still a child at heart who preferred the kids over "the grown-ups"), Sara loved spending time with her family. And as she shared story after story about them, it was easy to see where Sara learned to savor her moments and choose joy.

9 — 9 — 9

The kitchen, as in most homes, has always been the gathering place for my family. Some credit it to the smells of food wafting through the air, beckoning anyone and everyone to come and fulfill the curiosity their stomachs have forced upon them. Others say the kitchen is essential to a family because it's where the most time is spent preparing to formally sit and enjoy one another. Why wait to sit at the dining room table when you can sit on the kitchen counter, sneak samples of the cuisine, talk until everyone is trying to be just a shade louder than the others, lean on whichever counter Mom needs to be clear at the moment? This inevitably forced her comment, "We do have other rooms in the house, you know!"

But, of course, we all know deep down that the commotion would be missed, and she says now, sometimes with an edge of pride, that her family has grown up and the grandchildren are now carrying on the tradition. While all these are compelling reasons to hold the kitchen as the room of high esteem, none come close to competing with my mind's-eye view of my childhood in that old farm kitchen.

The hustle and chaos were ever-present. But no matter what the commotion, regardless if the television was blaring or the radio was silent, my dad would come up behind my mom—standing at the sink or stove or counter—and they danced. They danced. Dad would hum a tune or click out a beat and they would dance as though six children weren't running and talking and creating an atmosphere of Mardi Gras on Fat Tuesday.

They were experts in tuning out the world, until I came around. Until Dad felt that tug on his leg. Until Mom gave Dad the knowing grin and I was scooped up between them. Dad would have just showered and the smell of his aftershave would wash over our little circle of three. Mom would wink at me and we would begin the dance, the twirls, the spins. We would begin what I felt, but was too small to articulate, was my own world.

The dance would eventually end. The potatoes would boil on the stove or the phone would ring, and the universe would put my other little world on pause. But it was never on pause in my mind. Even today, when life seems overwhelming or uncertain, and that sense of security feels just beyond my reach, I can close my eyes and smell the smells of my youth. I see that old kitchen and my young parents, and I rest comfortably in the knowledge that at home in the new kitchen, my older parents are still dancing.

Those dances gave me security, taught me about love—and showed me how to live in the here and now. You should give it a try. In the midst of chaos, in the midst of fear, in the midst of uncertainty, in the midst of love, dance.

♪　♪　♪

Sara was the youngest of the Frankl kids, and though she spent many days in controlled chaos, running around with her sisters and brothers, she also enjoyed quieter days at home, alone with her mom. When she was too young to go to school like the other kids, Sara tagged along with her mom—who taught her, among so many other things, to look for the gifts in life.

9 — 9 — 9

Listening to the sound of the wind whistling around the building as the windows shook and the snow whipped into tiny volcanoes in and of itself, I found myself suddenly nostalgic for our farmhouse back on the acreage.

The blizzard here was just starting to get its footing. The winds were reaching their fifty miles per hour and the chill of the outside could be felt inside my bones. And then, for a moment, there was quiet. So I grabbed my camera and looked outside, knowing what I would see: sparkly snow, right outside my window.

It was always my favorite part of the storm, watching from the window with my mom. I can remember that night, being in the family room, watching television with the family, and suddenly noticing Mom was gone. I walked into the laundry room, knowing that's where I would find her. But there was no sloshing of a washer or tumbling of a dryer. It was quiet. Dark. And the only sound was that familiar whipping of the wind as she sat on a stool by the window, watching it swirl.

Her moment of silence in the peace of the white sparkly snow.

As an adult, I now recognize the quiet moment she was grabbing. A husband and six kids content in another room. Dishes done. The house vacuumed. No pressing for homework to be done or school clothes to be ready, because she knew the snow was only starting and our rural roads wouldn't be fit for the buses to pass.

She would sit quietly at the window and rest in the sound of the new-fallen snow. The peace in the wild whipping of the wind. I, of course, would break her silence, but only by my presence. I liked the quiet, too.

She would show me the light we were trying to see in the distance—the one a quarter mile away that lit up Dad's hog buildings. She was making sure the power was still on so the livestock were warm and fed and safe. But then she would take her eyes away from the light to make sure I saw the diamonds in the snow. She said they were the little gift that God gives in the middle of a storm.

And I would curl up with her on her stool and think about how she sparkled right along with them, in the quiet of the snow. There is no doubt that those little lessons then, about sparkly gifts in the middle of storms, help me to see the sparkle in my life now. Quietly content to watch the storms brew outside my windows—but only letting the sparkle rest inside.

9 — 9 — 9

To call Sara a daddy's girl seems like an understatement. She wrote about him often, calling him her first boyfriend and her valentine, and you could practically hear her smile through the computer screen when she told stories about his jokes and the way he loved to tease. Sara's blog name, "Gitzen Girl," even came from one of the many nicknames her dad had given her (a trait he passed on to her, as her young friends NieNie, Yodi, and Jonboy knew well).

When her dad suddenly passed away, Sara was heartbroken. The weeks and months following his death were full of dark days for her, both physically and emotionally, and the loss left a hole in her heart that never really healed. But even then, Sara searched until she found

joy. She held tight to the memories of her dad, and continued to
learn from his life. She shared with her readers lessons about being
intentional, serving others, and savoring moments instead of trying to
perfect them.

9 — 9 — 9

One year when I was a little girl, my dad gave me a ring for
Christmas. Someone—probably my mom—snapped a photo of
that moment, right there in Dad's office at the hog farm. I truly
have no idea why that would be the location he chose to put a
tiny little ring on my tiny little finger, but I love it because it
embodies the character of my dad.

He is a man who is filled to the brim with love. He's the guy
who would get on the floor to talk to you, who would be interested in your stories and would take the opportunity to tell you
how loved you are, what makes you special and what makes him
proud. He's also the dad who would tease you mercilessly, tickle
you until you begged for mercy, and climb trees to hang home-
made swings, only to get stuck trying to figure out how to climb
back down. He has always been a big kid, which made being his
kid a whole lot of fun.

I was too young to remember this Christmas, but I love the
photo that tells the story, the photo that wasn't taken under a
perfectly lit Christmas tree or when we were all dressed up to go
to church. I love that he stopped in the middle of his day, dressed
in his farm clothes—his snap-front shirt that surely had a pen
and a tiny notepad in the left front pocket and his smelly jeans
with a holder for his pliers on his hip—to let me know that I was
his girl. He knew how to savor his moments, and I'm so glad I
have the photo so I can look back and savor this moment, too.

9 — 9 — 9

Sara often savored her moments (her favorite things, remember) by
capturing them on camera. Her Canon Rebel was never far from her
side, usually in the basket of George (her walker). But sometimes she
got so busy living those moments that she forgot to take pictures—like
the time her brother, niece, and nephew stopped by for a visit. Even
if she never picked up her camera, though, Sara was undoubtedly
present when spending time with her loved ones, savoring every second
of her favorite times with her favorite people.

9 — 9 — 9

My brother and his kids made a quick trip home to my parents'
house last weekend—which was lovely for my parents but even
better for me because they pass right by my house on the way.
They came bearing McDonald's fries, accompanied by plenty of
hugs and smiles and stories to tell. Those kids absolutely steal
my heart every time I lay eyes on them. They were here for about
two hours, and I honestly was so focused on catching every word
they said and looking at those faces that change before my eyes
that (if you know me you know how insane what I'm about to say
is) I forgot to get out my camera.

I'm not kidding. They left and I about kicked myself. But then
I figured if I had remembered and taken the time to mess with
the camera, I probably would have missed a joke or smart-aleck
comment—and I decided to be thankful for forgotten photos and
savored moments.

Later that week my parents visited and then my sister Laura
stopped by. I unexpectedly got to see more family in the last week
and a half than I could have hoped to see at both Thanksgiving
and Christmas combined. It couldn't have worked out better if
we had planned it all—and I loved each moment.

As I sat talking with Laura about her amazing kids, I realized
how incredibly grateful I am that I savored my moments when I

had them. Back when I was able-bodied I was the youngest, the single one, the one with no attachments, so it was easy for me to travel around and keep in touch with everyone. If one of my siblings went home for the weekend with their kids, I went home, too, so I could see them. I traveled around to see a piano recital or a soccer game or simply to hang out. I couldn't get enough of the little people who had come into our family.

I had no idea that someday all of that wouldn't be possible anymore. I didn't know I was doing something smart back then. I wasn't living my life thinking, "What if?" I was just doing what I couldn't help but do: love the people in my family.

Ironically, the holidays aren't really that hard for me to miss out on. They're just holidays. What I hate missing is the sports and games, the first communions, the graduations, the recitals. I miss the lazy weekends with nothing on the schedule so we can play a game of marbles or make up stories before bed or watch *Harry Potter* movies back-to-back while eating all the ice cream in the house after the grown-ups have gone to sleep.

I don't like missing those things now but, people, I am so grateful I didn't miss them back then. Because I have savored moments that are irreplaceable to me. I've messed up things in my life, but this is one area of which I am thankful to have understood the importance.

You know that lyric, "You don't know what you've got 'til it's gone"? I've been so fortunate that sentiment hasn't seemed to apply to my life. I usually know how blessed I am to have what's right in front of me—like the years my brother's family lived here in town. Their house was close by and we had Sunday dinners, watched movies, went for walks, and enjoyed holidays together.

I knew exactly how good I had it when my nephew and niece were available to play or snuggle or go for a stroller ride. Today, when they visit, I soak up every last moment with them. And

they most certainly don't disappoint. They are never short on stories or ideas, and keep me thoroughly entertained.

I love that I have little traditions with the kids, and while it
was great to have Sunday dinners and stroller rides in years past,
I savor the stolen moments and excitement of getting to have
them visit now. I know exactly what I've got. And I love every
minute of it.

9 — 9 — 9

*When my daughter and I drove to visit Sara, I explained—again—
that Sara was sick and couldn't leave her house. I instructed my little
girl on manners and not being scared of Riley and a dozen other
rules a three-year-old couldn't possibly remember or follow. So when
my normally well-behaved daughter decided to open and shut every
door in Sara's condo and then proceeded to lock her bathroom door—
from the outside—I was mortified. We had locked Sara out of her
bathroom! Her only bathroom! In the house she couldn't leave!*

*I immediately began tripping over myself, apologizing and
brainstorming solutions—but Sara didn't panic or even get angry. She
just found a screwdriver for jimmying open the door and then asked
my daughter if she'd like to play with the teddy bear sitting on the
couch. As we drove home later that day—teddy bear in hand, because
Sara had insisted it come home with us—I thought that Sara had
more love for children than anyone I'd ever met. She loved kids with
her whole open heart—and they loved her, too.*

*Sara's friend Deb teaches first and second grade, and her students
adopted Sara a couple of years in a row—sending her cards and videos
and even collecting money to help pay for Sara's walker. Even long
distance, they fell in love with Sara—but that was nothing compared
to the kids in her family (or the ones she considered family). Her
friend Susie's son Jonathan called Sara his fairy godmother. Not to be
outdone, his younger brother Tyler gave Sara a newborn smile when*

she visited Susie at the hospital after he was born—a trip that resulted in Sara's being named Tyler's godmother, too, possibly because "Susie was afraid I would never give him back to her without some sort of claim on him."

Sara loved being a godmother, but aunt was by far her favorite role. Sara's sister live-streamed her son's and daughter's basketball games for her to watch from home, her friend Shannon videotaped her daughters' dance recitals for Sara, and when her friend Kelly told Sara she was giving her daughter a car for her sixteenth birthday, Sara insisted on creating signs for a scavenger hunt that ended in her parking lot, right outside her windows. She loved all of her kids with abandon, just the way they loved her.

9 — 9 — 9

As a single and childless woman, I have often been told by people that I just can't fully understand love for a child until I have one of my own. I have to tell you, though, a part of me feels very privileged to be in my position. No one is more important to me than my nieces and nephews. I have not, in my lifetime, felt a rush of love for my own child that is greater than my rush of love for them. I'm not their cousin's mom. I'm not looking out for someone ahead of them. Those ten people have the unconditional love and support of their parents, and when they aren't in the mood for that option they have an aunt who has no greater mission in life than to be their biggest supporter, their biggest cheerleader, and their most ardent fan. I am in their corner—and there's no place I'd rather be.

Actually, I think motherhood should come with a friend who is childless. I think what a mom sometimes wants is for another person to love her child with extreme abandon. A person who doesn't put another child in front of her own as a measuring stick.

Because let's be realistic: every mother thinks no child could possibly be more amazing than her own child. And she's right. Every single mother is right about that. Every child needs a mother who thinks they hung the moon, and every one of those mothers needs someone who will say, "You're totally right. Your child is absolutely that amazing!"

I get to be that person. And I love it.

When motherhood comes with a childless friend, you get to have someone to tell your woes to who won't tell you she has it worse with her own kids. You have someone to celebrate your child's accomplishment with, and the childless friend will think it's amazing because she has no frame of reference from which to judge it. You have someone you can share your concerns with and she won't tell you that you're overreacting, but instead hold your hand while you find out the answers.

Best of all, when you're a mother with a childless friend, you have someone who will love your child with every inch of her heart. Completely. Because she won't have her own to trump that space.

I admire each and every one of my friends with children. And I'm so grateful they let me be the childless friend they carry on their journey. Because I wound up being the childless friend with a life full of children—and it's been the joy of my life.

11

The Life You've Been Given

On How I Want to Be Remembered

Become all that God intended you to be.

Love Him. Love people. Love the life you've been given. —Based on Matthew 22:36–39

Faced with the knowledge that not only would her life never be "normal" or anything close to what she'd dreamed of, but also that it would likely be cut short, Sara could have easily focused on the injustice of her circumstances. Instead she chose to examine her heart and her life and to be intentional with her time, her gifts, her relationships, her words, her all. She carefully considered how she wanted to be remembered and then asked God to help her turn those desires into reality.

I had never heard of a life verse until recently. I know. The shock! But even though my friends and I all grew up in Christian households, no one I knew had ever heard of the concept either.

And then I joined the blogging world and people all talked about their life verses. How some had been given one by their parents, how others chose one for their baptism or confirmation, how some felt one had been spoken to them in some way.

But nothing had been speaking to me. I did, however, find a little treasure on the DaySpring site that I splurged on simply because it spoke to me as I assumed a life verse should. It reads, "Become all that God intended you to be. Love Him. Love people. Love the life you've been given." It sits by my bed so I see it all day—the words I want to live by. And while I could write volumes about each little part of each sentence, the word that continuously jumps out at me is *intended*.

God has an intention for me. My life here is not random.

Soak that in a minute. You aren't here just to get through life. You're not even here to succeed with your plans in life. No, you're here to fulfill what He has intended for you. It changes things, doesn't it?

I find myself looking at every moment and opportunity differently now. Life isn't about what I am in the mood for or what can fit into my day. Life is about being open to what He may need from me and what He has intended for me to notice. I'm here to keep my eyes and heart open enough to be aware of the moments in which He has intended for me to act.

Do you know what else it made me realize? That if He has intentions for my life, and has seen all that has happened and will happen, I don't have to worry about how I'll make it through. Because if I am still on this earth, it means He has intended for me to do something more. If I didn't have something more to do, He would reward me by taking me home to Him.

And that means He already knows I can make it through another day of this pain and illness. It means He already knows my family will survive the loss of my dad. It means He already knows I will survive whatever crosses my path today because He has intended for me to fulfill His purpose yet tomorrow.

I am a survivor. Not because I am strong or willful or unique. I am a survivor because God has intentions for me, and as long as I am here on this earth I have a job left to do. He saw that I would be sick, He saw that I would be devastated, He saw that I would feel weak—but He put me in this life because He also saw I would fulfill what He intended.

All I have to do is remember that this life isn't about me. It's about His intentions for me. If I trust Him with all of it—past, present, future—then He will make sure I am in the right position to fulfill all He intended.

Oh, and according to the life verse my friend helped me choose, I plan on doing it with joy. Habakkuk 3:18 says, "I will take joy"—and I will.

〃　〃　〃

I don't know anyone who enjoys writing their own bio. As Sara said, "You know, it's that short paragraph where you're supposed to sum up who you are and what you do. It's the place to give your credentials. But what happens when you don't have any credentials?" Her friend Holley knew Sara struggled with describing herself and said, "One thing I really appreciated about Sara was how she refused to be defined by anything, whether it was illness, or her life stage being single, or not having physical children. Any of those things. She just refused that and found joy in spite of those things." It would have been easy for Sara to throw herself a pity party and list off all the things she was not and all the things she did not do. But of course that wasn't her way. It may not fit into a tiny profile box, but Sara's answer to, "Who am I?" beautifully reveals exactly who she was.

〃　〃　〃

I don't have credentials. My old life had credentials, but it doesn't work to talk about who I was. I want to talk about who I am. Which begs the question: who in the world am I?

I'm the girl who loves with her whole heart.
I'm the girl who loves her friends' kids as if they were her own.
I'm the girl who would do anything for her family.
I'm the girl who believes her friends are her family.
I'm the girl who feels an intense bond with people she's never met in person.
I'm the girl who thinks her nieces and nephews are heaven-sent.
I'm the girl who loves to read and thinks music can take you out of your physical space.
I'm the girl who gets so lost in a story she forgets she's home.
I'm the girl who can't cook but always wanted to.
I'm the girl who knows her limitations, which is why she never tries to do math in her head.
I'm the girl who would rather listen than talk, but always has something to say.
I'm the girl who loves to write, and loves that she now has people on the other end of the computer screen to write to.
I'm the girl who will be more excited than you about your good fortune.
I'm the girl who struggles more with how this disease makes her look than how it makes her feel.
I'm the girl who is still convinced that she'll be able to accomplish tomorrow what she couldn't accomplish today.
I'm also the girl who will roll her eyes tomorrow when she realizes that she once again overestimated her capabilities.

I'm the girl who recognizes the huge blessing that comes in
the form of a little white pup.

I'm the girl who dreads disappointing people.

I'm the girl who can see the things she has lost aren't to
be mourned, but instead viewed as the blessings they
were.

I'm the girl who is grateful for being loved, not despite her
illness and limitations, but with them.

I'm the girl who will always believe in you, even when you
don't believe in yourself.

I'm the girl who is taking life as it comes, never leaving her
four walls, but living a complete life within them.

I'm the girl who will always choose joy.

*Sara readily admitted that she could be ornery, and anyone who spent
time with her knew that even on days when it physically hurt, she'd
often end up laughing so hard she snorted. I was never surprised to
have a conversation with or read a blog post from her that included
both a Bible verse and a quote from* Harry Potter *or* Friday Night
Lights. *Sara's words weren't always serious. But she did take her
words seriously.*

*Because she so valued God's purposes for her life and His designs
for who she was supposed to be, Sara was constantly examining her
life and her words, asking if they lined up with Truth, if they truly
represented her heart and God's intentions. Sometimes her life or her
heart had changed enough that she needed to revise her words, but
other times her words served as a reminder of what she believed and
valued, what was true and enduring.*

A section of my bio on my blog says I'm "learning that home-bound doesn't limit your life, just your location." And it's been taunting me a bit lately.

Of course, the way I meant it is still true. I still mean that, through this blog and the Internet and the phone and the mail, I get to touch people's lives and they flood mine with beauty and grace. It's true that my location doesn't matter when it comes to community. I am so grateful for that.

It's not the homebound part that feels like it's limiting my life these days; it's life itself.

A few months ago, my nurse suggested we have physical ther-apy start coming to the house again for a short period of time. I had to stop doing any sort of therapy when Cushing's hit, and my abilities have changed fairly drastically since then. I thought it would be a great idea to have someone come in and refresh me on what I should be doing.

The key here is that I thought I'd still be able to do it. Do some-thing. Do anything. But I can do nothing. My physical therapist went from talking about exercises to saying that my goal should be getting out of bed periodically and walking to the kitchen and back. I was ready for stretches and lifts and maybe some stretchy bands. Turns out, I can barely move my ankles without them swelling. Forget about the rest of me.

I had the same wake-up moment when my friend Nicole and her girls came last weekend. I knew I would be in bed most of the time, but I thought I would at least get up and sit on the couch a little or sit at the table during a meal here and there. But after sitting at the table with them for all of fifteen minutes, I was barely able to make it back to the bedroom without passing out. By the time they left for the hotel that night I was shaking and vomiting from trying to be "active" earlier.

It broke my heart. It broke my spirit. It was in that moment that I came face-to-face with something I knew to be true but had been trying so hard to make false. I had moved from feeling like a sick person to feeling like an invalid. And I hate it.

Admittedly, I am fighting an infection, but fighting infections has become my norm more than a random event. When I am here alone, I do nothing but stay in bed, rest, do little bits on the computer here and there, and try my best to exist with a good attitude. I can get by on my own, get to the kitchen and back, bathroom and back. I am safe and capable. But that is it. Throw some people and activity in there, and I can't accomplish even that. Activity for me is now defined as sitting up in bed and talking and being animated. Talking now requires a nap. I have no stamina.

It's like a dagger to my heart every time I have these realizations. Every time I see myself physically slipping to another level—the invalid level.

But I have to look at it, otherwise I constantly set my sights on things higher than I can achieve, and I end in failure. I have to recognize my limitations so I don't end up making myself worse because I'm trying to make my life into something it isn't. God is telling me to live the life He's given me, not the life I'm trying to wish into existence.

My perspective has to come from a still space in this bed. It has to come after long rests and acceptance of where I am. If there is a purpose for me on this earth, and there must be because I am still here, then I need to keep my eyes open to the here and now and find it where I am.

I am feeling like an invalid these days. And I hate it. But I know He sees more in me than my location. He will not let my life be in-valid.

❧ — ❧ — ❧

As Sara dealt with the frustration of her limitations, she read about the origins of her name. I can almost hear her response even now: "Are you kidding me?!" The painfully coincidental meaning threw her for a loop as she wrestled with God, trying so hard to figure out what in the world He was telling her. The conclusion she finally came to took my breath away—and taught me, again, the value of digging deep to find the gift and choose the joy.

𝄞   𝄞   𝄞

Recently I was reading Angie Smith's book *I Will Carry You.* In one part where she discusses the story of Abraham and Isaac, she looks up the origins of the word *trial.* It turns out *trial* is from the Hebrew word *sara,* which means "to bind, tie up, restrict." Angie's book says that the noun *trial* therefore denotes a narrow place where one is bound or restricted.

I read that, and then read it again. And as I tried to digest it, I kept muttering to myself, "God, what are You trying to say here?!?!"

My name, Sara, means to be in a narrow place in life where one is bound or restricted. Me. Sara. Who is homebound. Restricted by my location. Restricted by my very body that can barely move from the pain. Restricted by my lungs that don't allow a deep breath anymore. Restricted from life beyond my four walls.

I got it. Not subtle. But what point was God trying to make? What's the point? That's usually a question I try to avoid. I don't ask, "What's the point of all this, of my illness, my pain, my limitations?" I avoid the question because I'm fully aware I may never know the answer. I may never know how He is choosing to use my life or why not healing me fits into His plan. And I decided a long time ago that it's okay if I never know, because I trust Him. He knows, and that's all that matters.

But as I sat there and wondered about this meaning of the

word and my name, it occurred to me that as my physical life has been made narrow, as I have been bound and restricted and faced this trial, He has saved me from living a narrow life.

Because of this trial, my world—my life—has been opened up to a community that has stepped forward to share my life, my story, my faith. I have been stretched and pulled and reshaped in my beliefs. My life has been fuller and deeper and wider, maybe not despite my homebound status, but because of it.

My name is the origin of the word *trial*. I am bound and restricted. But He saved me from living a narrow life. He took my trial and redeemed it. I thought, as Isaac, I was not spared because I am not healed. But in truth, He healed my spirit. And set me free.

9   9   9

I don't think Sara had any idea how many people's lives she touched and changed, how many people she inspired and ministered to. As her journey came to a close, hundreds spoke about the effect Sara had on them. It's interesting, then, to read of her desire to be a living prayer and of her respect for one who changed the world. Sara may not have changed the entire world but she certainly changed my world and so many others'.

9   9   9

I've never really given much thought to the type of things I want people to say at my funeral. I tend to focus more on how I'm living right now and hope that how I'm remembered falls in line because of it. That changed a bit this August when Eunice Kennedy Shriver passed away.

In a statement by the family, they described her as "a living prayer, a living advocate, a living center of power. She set out to change the world and to change us, and she did that and more."

That phrase has stuck with me, and I think often about what it means to be described as a living prayer.

I tried to imagine what that might look like in a tangible application, but I couldn't. I've decided that kind of a life wouldn't be seen in a look or a stature. What I've decided instead is that it would be found in the reflection of others when they are touched by you. It would be seen in the joy that others find contagious, in the compassion that others feel in your words and deeds. It would be found in the empathetic nature of a stranger and in the fortitude seen in those who are determined to make a difference. The kind word for no reason, the intentional way of listening, the hand outstretched to give and to receive, the voice of encouragement, the touch of comfort, the openness to share in word and deed—all of these things must be what a living prayer looks like to others.

All we can really do in life is be open to what God needs from us, to be aware and present in our circumstances so we are available to step up when called. Now, though, thinking about how I want to be remembered is helping me choose my daily actions. I want to be a living prayer.

Socrates is credited with the statement, "The unexamined life is not worth living." Sara's life, obviously very much worth living, was also far from unexamined. She never rested on her laurels; she never coasted. She constantly examined and looked inward and upward to make sure she continued living the life God had called her to. As she began her last year and looked heavenward often, she became even more determined not to miss a single blessing or purpose God had for her in this life.

Imagine if we all went about our lives remembering the core of who we are: a Spirit born in the image of Christ who is sent here to fulfill a purpose before going back home.

I forget that so easily. I want to make this life all about me. All about my human existence instead of my spiritual being. I want to worry about my health and my finances and my housing and my potential. I want less pain and more easy. I want I want I want.

But what I have is a mission. A purpose. I am here to live the best life I can with what I have been given. I am here to live out this human existence as a spiritual being—a servant to God and His people—before I head back home to Him.

I'm not worried about starting over in a new year. I'm not worried about what this year might bring. I am simply keeping in mind that this life isn't about me and my goals and my wants and my worries. I am here to fulfill His purpose for me, and my job is to keep my eyes open so I don't miss it.

12

God Is Awake

On Living and Dying Well

❧ ❧ ❧ ❧ ❧

Have courage for the great sorrows of life and patience for the small ones.

And when you have finished your daily task, go to sleep in peace. God is awake. —Victor Hugo

After Sara began receiving hospice care near the end of her life, her family was with her. Her sister shared, "Sara's focus was on making sure those of us left here on earth were taken care of. That we were okay. She said, 'I'll be fine. Isn't this exciting? I want to make sure you're okay...' She was so courageous. Without shedding a tear, and filled with joy, she told us how excited she was to meet our Heavenly Father. Even in those last days, she continued teaching us—how to love, how to be brave, how to choose joy."

❧ ❧ ❧

This quote by Victor Hugo is my all-time favorite. Something about it grounds me and instantly makes me feel like I've taken a deep breath. When I read it, everything in my body relaxes a little as it reminds me to hand over my burdens and teaches me to trust. It has taught me that I have a well of courage and fortitude inside of me for when trials beat on my door unceasingly. It also gives me instructions for when to take action in my life and when to let go of the notion that I have any control or power.

It's written on my wall of doodles, and I only have to turn my head a little to the left to see it while I'm on the computer. I find myself looking to my left often to read what has become my mantra of sorts.

It's a bit ironic because sleep is not when I am most peaceful. Most people love crawling into bed at night and disappearing into a world where no one is telling them about their deadlines or reminding them of the incomplete to-do lists that inevitably await. You may slip into bed and fall asleep when your head hits the pillow, or take a few moments at the end of your day to enjoy the blissful silence of the night. Maybe you escape into the pages of a good book or whisper about your day to the love of your life lying next to you.

Or maybe you just collapse from exhaustion and pray the sound of the alarm clock holds off until you are fully rested and ready to face a new day. Either way, many find nighttime to be a welcome reprieve.

For me, as much as I try to change my mind-set about it, it's mired in dread. Pain plays many tricks on the body but the worst for me is that it's not conducive to rest or sleep. All of the remedies of relaxation, turning off the television, and creating an atmosphere of rest go out the window when pain is involved. No amount of rest in the mind can counteract the reality of aching joints and pressured bones when one is lying down. So my two worst times of the day are getting into bed at night and having to get myself out of it in the morning. With sleep medications and muscle relaxers I find moments of sleep in the night. And I appreciate every little moment I get.

The part I appreciate the most about this quote is the knowledge that through all of my nighttime struggles, God is awake. Even in pain I am able to rest without fear and worry because I have finished what God asked of me that day, and because He never sleeps. He is awake, walking the path I will take tomorrow so that He can show me the smoothest way through the dark valleys. So He can lead me by the restful waters that He has placed on my path. So He can restore my soul.

I can rest because He is awake. And knowing that brings me peace. That feeds my joy. That allows me to accept my life. That lets me move forward when forward seems crazy.

9 — 9 — 9

Resting easy, like choosing joy and focusing on gratitude and pursuing community, didn't come without a fight. But what made the process of learning to rest while trusting God hardest was that it required putting down her boxing gloves and walking away from the fight. For Sara—a vital young woman full of life and strength and determination—that was counterintuitive and hard to learn.

9 — 9 — 9

The early days of this disease were not easy. They were less painful and limiting, but no less scary. Suddenly dealing with pain and limitations and the unknown of what could come were unsettling at best. But knowing what I should do about it? That was the easy part. I knew to fight.

I knew to fight through pain, I knew to fight doctors until someone did the right thing, I knew to research and arm myself. I knew to fight to keep my life.

I had to do things differently to keep it. I had to do physical therapy and try experimental options and grasp at every straw. I took correspondence courses when I couldn't sit in three-hour seminars at college, but I still graduated. I sang at church, but went to the lobby to lie on the couches during the sermon so I could have the energy to go in and finish singing the rest of the service. But I still sang. I adjusted everything in my life so that life—in essence—could stay the same. I knew how to fight.

I did my research and knew what could come, so instead of giving in to the pain I fought to stay mobile. I moved when it hurt. I forced myself to lie flat when my bones would barely straighten. I would lie on my stomach for forty minutes every night when I first got into bed to try to keep a straight spine. Even when I wanted to scream. I knew it was important. So I fought.

Even when I had to give things up, I was giving them up in order to fight. I gave up my job so I could stay out of the hospital. I gave up dreams so I could keep from getting sicker. Every move I made to do fewer of life's activities was me fighting to keep my life. Fighting to stay social with my friends and keep my environment steady so my sanity was steady.

Now, though, the more I fight, the sicker I get. The more I try, the less I am able. The more I do what I know, the more it slips through my fingers. I did all that fighting and yet now find myself mostly confined to my bed. And not in that straightened position I fought so hard to maintain. I've just had to have the conversation with my friends—whose kids get sick and coworkers cough and schools are filled with cases of croup—where I tell them that my door has to stay shut to them until the season of health comes back around. I fought to stay active in their lives, and now I have to physically keep them out of mine.

To keep my body safe, to fight to not be sicker after a year and a half straight of Cushing's and constant infections, I have to give up the things I was fighting for.

And now? I'm learning as I go to let it go. I'm learning to live in this different version of life, to rest and not fight—because fighting no longer seems to always be the answer. I spent years fighting—and the fighting turned out to be more exhausting than the accepting. Accepting what is, living with it, embracing it, and finding joy in it is the only way I know to live a productive life. And as much as this disease has taken from me, it's also given to me and taught me and strengthened me.

I've learned (over and over) that being tough and being strong are two completely different things. I just had to stop being tough and start being strong to figure it out. Now I'm strong enough to live the life I've been given instead of the one I think I'm tough enough to make. Back when I had a job and a social life outside this condo, I didn't live my life; I pushed through my life trying to get to one I wanted instead, one that didn't exist. I was fighting, being tough. But I've found a strength in letting go that I wouldn't trade for anything—no matter how many times I have to relearn the lesson.

ঌ — ঌ — ঌ

As her pain increased and her health deteriorated, Sara's strength was more and more in letting go of her fight and leaning on God. The lie many of us believe—that we can handle everything, that we can go it alone—only keeps us from moving forward. Admitting that life is overwhelming, asking for help and accepting it: these are the ways we become stronger. Not heroic and not on our own, but by acknowledging our frailty and our need, we leave room for God to work in us and give us strength. Sara knew this, and she made sure her readers knew, too, that our job isn't to take care of everything but instead to give thanks even when life is too much, and to lean on the One Who is big enough to handle it all.

❧ ❧ ❧

Sometimes I get overwhelmed. My disease has been on a steady decline and it has taken most of my energy with it. And it is easy in these moments of hard to get overwhelmed. To wonder where the energy for the next moment will come from. It's easy to let the pain of today and the unknown of tomorrow take what energy is there and waste it away.

I wonder sometimes if, in some small way, that is how Jesus felt in that garden when He was sweating blood over what was to come. If in the moment of hard it was easy for Him to be overwhelmed, too, despite knowing and believing in and loving His Father.

And then I remember that even though He did get overwhelmed, even though He did ask for the cup to pass Him by as I so often want to do, He did something else in the middle of it all that night. He took action. He gave thanks at the Last Supper. With a dread that must have been filling the heart of Man, He took what He had left of His life and gave thanks. And then He shared it with all who were there with Him.

Jesus took the pain that was to come for Him and, in the midst of what must have been overwhelming, acknowledged the Father. He acknowledged that what was going to be brutal for Him would be transformed into grace, because that is what the Father does. He didn't let what would overwhelm Him in the garden overshadow the beauty He trusted would come: a beauty that only God can bring from the hard.

God wants to transform our hard the same way. We all know

how God turned the pain of Jesus's journey into joy for each of us. And it all started with an action, not just Jesus saying yes, but Jesus giving thanks.

And so, as I lie in the quiet with my own pain, feeling the natural inclination to be overwhelmed, I take action as He did. I give thanks for the gifts that come from pain. I give thanks for the people and the moments and the experiences. I give thanks to a Savior Who was willing to go through the pain so that the hard I live through could also be redeemed. I give thanks even when I don't easily see the gifts, because I trust that He is making beauty in places my eyes can't see. Because that is where I find my joy.

9 — 9 — 9

In the months before Sara passed away, she became more reflective. She still stayed focused on the present, trusting her future to God and expressing thanks for everything He had done and would do. But as she continued grieving the loss of her father, her heart turned toward eternity and things everlasting. Her friend Lisa-Jo said, "When I talked to Sara, I knew Jesus was in the room. I think it's because Sara wasn't afraid of talking about a lot of things that the rest of us are scared of. We don't like to even say the word die or dying. When I got to know Sara, it really was in the last few months of her life. She was dying, and she knew it. The remarkable thing about her is that she stood with one foot firmly planted here, and another foot firmly planted in Heaven, and she was ready to go there. What was remarkable about her is that she wasn't afraid to go, and she was being brave to stay." Sara wrote the following essay about the unknown in response to a prompt on Lisa-Jo's blog.

9 — 9 — 9

I have lived in this condo since I was twenty-nine years old. I haven't left it, ventured out, even opened a window in years. It's where I am, where I will always be, and yet when someone says the word *home* I don't think here. I don't think anywhere, really. I think whom. Because my home rests in the hearts of people. My home is not here. It's not in a country or state or town or walls. It's in the hearts of the people I love. It's with friends who are near and loved ones who are far. It's with people I've shared my life with but may never meet face-to-face, until we all go to our final home. And I'm excited for the day I return home, even though it's an unknown.

The unknown can be our biggest enemy sometimes, the thing we focus on and spend most of our energy trying to control.

I sometimes wonder if it's actually more comforting for us to look ahead and live in the future and all the unknown simply because we feel a desperate need to avoid the present we're in. Because, let's face it, the present can be hard. We can be broke or we can be sick or we can be abandoned. We can be living in limbo in our marriages or in crisis with our jobs or aching for our children and their needs. The right now can hurt so badly that the only escape is to get lost in the unknown of those "what-ifs" that give us the illusion of control.

What if I take this job, or what if we lose the house, or what if we make that move, or what if I get the raise, or what if I try this treatment?

We can live in fear and dread the unknown, assuring ourselves of the worst—or we can live in hope and see happiness ahead with Pollyanna eyes. But neither is truly right. Both are still guessing games of the unknown.

I'm learning how to fully live right in the middle of the hard, in the here and known, because if this is my life, if this is where I am—then this is where God is, too. And if I'm wasting all of my time and energy trying to control the unknown of the future rather than fulfilling what He may need from me right now, then

I'm wasting God's time as well. It all boils down to this: none of it is unknown to Him.

ꝯ——ꝯ——ꝯ

Though Sara had been very sick for a while (on top of her "normal" sick, a term Sara called the understatement of the year), her final days came quickly, before she could write any last words on her blog. Friends and family kept Sara's online community updated as she became sicker, entered hospice care, and passed away. Those of us miles away and spread across the map held our breaths waiting for those updates, praying and hoping. During that last week—and the days following her death—it seemed as if our whole corner of the Internet linked virtual arms and circled our Sara.

But what we felt was just a fraction of the grief those walking with Sara felt on the last leg of her journey. Of course, even then, Sara's first concern was for others, and she worried about their sadness and made time to speak blessings and love to each one of her friends and family members there. Her sister Laura describes those final days.

ꝯ——ꝯ——ꝯ

When Sara called and asked me to come, she said, "Don't worry. I'm okay, I was just wondering if you could come be with me."

Sara always loved to have people come visit, but she rarely asked. Sometimes it was because she wasn't feeling well, but mostly she didn't want to be a burden to anyone. Typically, if I was going to visit, I had to be the one to tell her I was coming. I only recall one other time she asked me to come because she needed help. It was when her disease, her pain, was more than she could handle. She had Cushing's, she needed the doctors' help, and she couldn't get to them.

So even though she said, "Don't worry," I did nothing on that four-hour trip but worry and pray, asking God to please show me how to help my sweet sister.

I knew this time was different. Sara's health had been getting worse. She had just received IVs the weekend before because of dehydration. As I drove, I thought of the necklace Sara gave me that says, "By Grace Alone." I always wear it, and I needed God's grace so badly that day. Without His grace, I was lost. How was I going to help her? How could I ease her suffering and pain?

When I walked through the door of her condo, Sara's dear friend Meg was with her, sitting next to her in bed. I hugged Sara (as much as I could without creating more pain) and I said, "Is this time different?" She said, "Yes, I think so." We cried, Meg left, and throughout that night I helped her as she struggled constantly. She hardly had a moment without relief from pain and getting physically sick.

Morning finally came and her friend and home nurse Tabetha came to see how Sara was doing. After she saw Sara, we had much conversation, blood tests were taken, the results were received, and the words came: "You may want to consider hospice."

My tear-filled eyes met Sara's and she said, "YES."

My head said, "NO," but my heart felt hers as excitement filled her face. Sara was finally going to meet our Heavenly Father. She said, "Yes." And so she began her journey to be with our Heavenly Father and our dad.

For the first time in as long as I can remember, Sara was provided with enough medication to ease her pain and keep her from getting physically sick. As we watched the medication begin to work, we also saw the many years of pain leave her face. She looked like an angel—an angel ready for her journey to Heaven.

Over her last few days, while she was in hospice care, Sara took time
to speak with each one of her close friends and family. Her friend Meg
shared, "She was so calm and she was so ready. She just knew that
she was going to a better place and to be able to be reunited with her
dad. Having that conversation with her lying in the bed is something
I will never, ever forget. I hope that when it's my time that I will be
like her." Sara also spoke with her siblings, sending messages to her
beloved nieces and nephews during that time, to make sure they were
okay. Taking care of the people she loved before she left them was, as
her mom said, Sara's final mission.

৯ — ৯ — ৯

In keeping with Sara's motto, "It's not about me," over the
course of the next two days, her focus was on making sure those
of us left here on earth were taken care of, that we were okay.
And she was so courageous! Without shedding a tear, and filled
with joy, she told us how excited she was to meet our Heavenly
Father. She continued teaching us. Teaching us how to love,
choose joy, and be courageous.

Our hearts grieve over her loss, but we are so grateful and our
spirits rejoice over what she has left us. She has left us so much
of herself through her writings and the life she lived. The life she
lived for God and others! For this we will be forever grateful. We
will always love Sara—all the way around the world and back
and, now, into the heavens.

৯ — ৯ — ৯

Friends of Sara traveled from every corner of the country to say
goodbye at her memorial service and funeral. And for those who
couldn't make it, the services were live-streamed online and recorded
for later viewings as well. One of Sara's best friends, Alece, had visited
Sara several times after they connected online. She shared words of

love and joy at Sara's memorial service, echoing both the grief and the gratitude so many were feeling.

❧　❧　❧

There are so many things I could say about my sweet Sara. So many that I don't even know where to start. Or harder still, I wouldn't even know where to stop. She has been one of the greatest gifts in my life, and her friendship has truly changed me. Forever.

And I know many—literally around the world—can say the exact same thing about her. It is absolutely mind-blowing to think of how far-reaching Sara's impact has been. From the tiny confines of her condo in Iowa, her life and love wrapped around the globe. Because of her illnesses, her way of life had to change. But her way of living didn't.

Sara continued to live well. To love deeply. To trust God unswervingly. She continued to choose joy. To love Jesus passionately. And to run her race well…all the way to the end.

Through her words, Sara shared her faith and her heart so genuinely and authentically. Sara was real. *Velveteen Rabbit* kind of real. And in her realness, she made it easy for us to be real in return. Real with ourselves, with others, with God.

And in that place of threadbare honesty, she challenged us to choose joy.

Choose joy. Those two words ran deep for Sara. They weren't just a pick-me-up statement; those words truly shaped her life.

Sara taught me that choosing joy doesn't mean living in denial of reality. It doesn't mean pretending everything is okay when it's not. It doesn't mean not allowing ourselves to grieve or acknowledge our own heartaches in life. It means being honest and authentic with where we are and, from that place, still lifting our eyes homeward.

Choosing joy is acknowledging that while I don't understand what's going on, God does. Choosing joy is remembering that while life seems to be spiraling out of control, it is never out of God's control. Choosing joy is remaining mindful that while my circumstances may feel anything but ideal, God still has my good and His glory in mind. Because like Sara said, "It's not about me. It's about what He can do with my life." That statement holds the very essence of her lifestyle of choosing joy.

Sara lived well. She loved well. She finished well. And she taught us to do the same.

ɔ ——ɔ ——ɔ

Before Sara died, she asked her friend Shannon to speak at her wake. Opinionated to the end, she told Shannon that she should talk about who Sara had been, so people could really see her. And she informed Shannon as well that she was not allowed to cry because it would "make things less effective." Oh, Sara. I'm not sure there was a dry eye left after Shannon spoke; I know mine weren't. But I also know that anyone who heard the beautiful tribute below surely saw the Sara we all knew and loved, the Sara whose legacy would live long past that fall day, the Sara who touched so many and inspired us all to live well and to choose joy.

ɔ ——ɔ ——ɔ

Words are powerful, uniting. They shape our view of the world, ourselves, each other. Words, in the best cases, make us immortal. Words are how I found her. Faith is what brought us together.

A friend sent me an e-mail, asking me to pray for a mother who knew she was going to lose her baby girl and carried her to term anyway. I immediately prayed, and then got online to read something called a blog. It was the first time I'd read one—in my life. I took in the entries from first to last, with tears streaming. My heart ached. I prayed. I returned again and again to follow this mom's story. And in the process? I found Sara.

Our friendship was wildly unexpected. I linked to gitzengirl .blogspot.com and as I read I heard her voice: honest, full of faith, strong, true. Her words? They were her, and like a book waiting to be opened, I dove in. Heart-first. Because that's how all of the great things in life are to be done.

I sent an e-mail explaining the similarities in our stories and assuring her that I'd never written to someone like this before, I wasn't creepy, and um, if she had some time, could we possibly correspond? She immediately replied with, "Of course! I'd love to get to know you!" And, as it's said, the rest, for us, was history. Day in, day out, "doing life" together. Only now, knowing what I do about her, does this response make me laugh. I'm quite sure that is how Sara answered every single person who contacted her.

Sara did everything full throttle, both feet in, filled with intention and limitless enthusiasm, shown by the sparkle in her eyes for what most interested those she loved. She told me once that the most important gift you could give someone was your full and undivided attention. Sara knew that to live well meant to treasure moments and see them as gifts. She chose joy. Not happiness, which is as flimsy as a shirt blowing on a line in the breeze, but true heart joy, which sustains through obstacles, disease, death. She made the hard choices—every day.

Sara chose community, using her words to a build a life when her body failed her. She shared her faith boldly. She was real, alive, present in every moment. She made those around her and those who shared her world desire to enjoy their days as she would have: no going back, no regrets, and taking the time to feel the sun kiss their cheeks and cause freckles, which she so missed seeing on her own. Sara lived. Every single day.

She was a daughter, a sister, a friend. She loved to sing. She loved to dance. She made the world's best volcano cake. She adored cheese and Oreos, frozen and dipped in peanut butter. Some have called her inspirational. She was, but not intentionally. Honestly, though? To me? She's simply Sara, my best friend. The one with the snort-filled laugh who made up songs for everything. She had eyes that twinkled and hugs that filled you up way past overflowing. She was my heart.

And here she is, proclaiming that it's not about her, in full Sara-gets-the-last-word fashion. But this time? I have to disagree. Because it is about her, what He's done through her. It's about her taking the time to teach us through her words and her beautiful life how to be genuine and honest. How to love the Lord and follow Him. How to make our lives more outwardly focused than in-. Loving well. Living well. Choosing joy. That was our Gitz. And because here, in this place, she deserves the final word, I'll leave you with hers: "Make it about Him, not you. Enjoy every second. Choose joy."

Well said, good and faithful servant. Well said.

Acknowledgments

Sara's Family

Our gratitude ultimately is to God, our Father. By wholly trusting in Him, the journey to fulfill a dream of Sara's came true. One of the last things Sara said before going home to her Heavenly Father was, "I want people to continue learning, believing, and trusting in God as I sought to be God's disciple. But it's not about me; it's about Him. That is the message I want people to hear."

Gratitude must also be extended to Sara's extended family, friends, and blog community. The unconditional love and support each of you showed Sara made it possible for her dreams of independence, being in community, and feeling a sense of "home" without leaving the four walls of her condo to come true. Her dream was possible because her home was in each of your hearts.

Mary Carver

One of my favorite things to do, especially when I arrive at a particularly significant or momentous occasion, is to think back to how the whole thing got started. Following the bread crumbs of decisions and actions, of conversations and connections, is fun for me; I find something so satisfying about seeing the journey from the perspective of my destination. But life isn't really a choose-your-own-adventure book, and no path taken is ever as straightforward as it might appear. So the best part of reaching the end of this book's creation is realizing how many people, how many choices, how many factors completely out of my control led me here—and how many amazing twists and turns are probably just around the corner.

Thank you to every single person who played a part in this journey. I am overwhelmed with gratitude and humbled by the incredible opportunity to share Sara's story with the world.

My first thanks must go to Sara's family. Thank you for trusting me with Sara's words and her legacy. Thank you for praying with me and sharing your lives with me. I will forever be grateful for your friendship and your trust.

Thank you to my parents, who taught me from the very beginning that words matter. I am a word girl because I am your girl.

Thank you a million times over to my husband, my very favorite person. Mark, you have given me the most beautiful gift by believing in my dreams. You don't even hesitate; you just believe I can do what I'm called to do. You also keep my crazy in check and pick up dinner when the babies and books overwhelm me. Thank you. I love you. A lot.

And thank you to Annalyn, who cheered on her mom with deadline countdowns, bedtime prayers, and more grace and understanding than I deserve. You are a word girl in your own right, and I cherish your sweet encouragement so much.

Thank you to Sandi, for listening to me talk on and on about books and writing and publishing and blogging every Friday night after dinner. I might not remember inviting you to my sixth birthday party, but I'm so glad you came—that day and every day since then.

I could not have faced or finished this book without the women who prayed for me. Not only have you sincerely encouraged me to write over the years but when I asked you to pray for this book at this time, you did it without hesitation and without ceasing. Thank you for lifting me up. Thank you for being generous with your prayers and your encouragement. I love you all.

The world of blogging is a strange one, that's for sure, but I am eternally grateful for the friendships it has given me. Thank you to my (in)courage sisters for loving Sara so well and cheering for our book, for answering my questions big or small, and for being for me. I am for you, too.

I'm also so thankful for my Sisterchicks, another group of blogging sisters that has seen me through some of the darkest and brightest days of my life. Thank you, especially, to Amanda (for meaning it when you said this would be our year to make art and for believing that God made me to write books) and Jill (for giving me tough love when I get lost in my head, fashion tips when I'd rather wear sweats, and an outlet for my deepest thoughts about Veronica Mars and Taylor Swift).

Huge thanks to Dawn, who connected the dots on this book's map. Who would have thought that standing in line together at a conference to meet an agent would lead us here?! Thank you for your encouragement to Make the Call Already, and thank you for sharing your agent with Sara's family and me. I'm so glad we're on this publishing road together, sweet friend.

And thank you to Ruth Samsel, my literary agent and personal cheerleader. Thank you for taking a chance on me, for reminding me that I can do this, and for holding my hand as I braved the world of publishing.

Thank you to my wonderful editor and team at FaithWords. Your passion for this project and belief in Sara's message has transformed an idea into a legacy. Thank you for partnering with us.

Finally and most of all, I'm exceedingly grateful to God for using this book to change my heart with His grace, His goodness, and His love. He is the Author of Sara's and my stories, and the way He's woven them together is beautiful.

Appendix

Tributes to Sara

I have fought the good fight, I have finished the race,
I have kept the faith.

Now there is in store for me the crown of righteousness,
which the Lord, the righteous Judge, will award to me
on that day—and not only to me, but also to all who
have longed for his appearing.   —2 Timothy 4:7–8 (NIV)

*Sara passed away on September 24, 2011, after receiving hospice care
for eleven days. During that time her body was finally able to rest and
she was surrounded by friends and family hoping to bless her as she
had spent her life blessing them. It's no exaggeration to say that when
this news reached the blogging community of which Sara had been
such a vital, vibrant member, she was mourned around the world.
But even in this there was joy. As Sara's friends from social media
struggled to say goodbye, some to a person they'd never met yet felt so
connected to, her message of hope and joy spread even farther than
ever.*

*Over the week and a half Sara was in hospice care, her family read
to her messages sent via e-mail, text, and Facebook, as well as blog
posts written in her honor. Like so much of Sara's life, her last days
were a bittersweet mix of joy, relief, pain, and grief—but never regret.
Sara lived every moment she was given wholeheartedly and with a
full faith. And though those who loved her were incredibly sad to say
goodbye, they knew Sara was finishing her journey well and heading
home to be reunited with both her earthly father and her Heavenly
Father.*

ϑ—ϑ—ϑ

Sara was the most real person I've ever known. She was light.
She was Jesus to people. The real, in-the-flesh, no-holds-barred
Jesus. The one that walked with sinners.

She had a wicked sense of humor and snorted when she
laughed. Her marker collection was the largest I've ever seen not
in a Crayola display. She loved *Alias* and wanted Jennifer Garner's
arms. She froze her Oreos. She loved Sonic lime slushes. She
taught Riley to use the bathroom indoors. She loved movies, all
kinds. Even if she didn't like a gift she'd put it on immediately.
She liked to feel dressed even when lying in bed. She was never
scared to tell me the truth, even if I didn't want to hear it. She
colored her hair and it never turned out the color she wanted it
because of its red undertones. And she was way too big and full
of light to be of this world.

Joy. I'm choosing it. Now. In this moment. Through the tears,
the pain, the memories. In loving Sara, I've made my choice.
I choose joy.

—*Shannon Hayward*

Our friendship has been such a beautiful blessing. Never in
a million years would I have expected a sweet blog commenter

to become like family to me. But that is exactly what she has become. Sara is like family to me. She is the biggest gift this blog has brought me.

Selfishly, I am not ready for her to go. But I know God is calling her home and that her legacy will live for generations. She has taught me so much about what it means to run the race well and glorify the Lord in all circumstances.

Even though she was just in my life for a couple years, I'm a better person because of her, because she loved well. She chose joy. She chose to love well, to love fully, to be that friend who picked up the phone and went shopping for baby girl headbands on Etsy with me, and also just dove into a real relationship. I think that people think that online friendships can't be real, can't be deep—but Sara proves that wrong. My life is better, and thousands of people's lives are better, because of Sara's story.

—*Jessica Turner*

Sara taught me how to choose joy. She taught me that regardless of what is going on, there is another perspective, a choice about how you look at your surroundings. Are you going to dwell on the negative and the things that really are out of your control and you cannot change? Or are you going to take aspects of that and see how you can embrace who you are, what your abilities are in that moment to take that situation and just run with it and live with it in joy? Sara had joy. People can look at her and say, "There's no way. How can she have joy?" But she had joy. She knew what joy was.

—*Tam Hodge*

Grief and joy often reside together. And no one modeled that for me better than Sara. Despite illness, pain, and so much loss, she made the continual decision to choose joy. I'm not talking about a plastic facade of happiness. Sara had the kind of genuine joy that comes from the simple but oftentimes hard decision to trust that God remains in control even when everything is spiraling out of control.

In her life and also in her death, Sara taught me lifetimes' worth about trusting Jesus, loving well, and choosing joy. I know she did the same for so many around the world. Being homebound only extended Sara's reach, and thousands of people have continued to embrace and live out her mantra: *Choose joy.*

—*Alece Ronzino*

Sara's song has been singing years before I met her online. Even though she was sick, her spirit was not bound by walls. Her song of joy, through her words, leaped free and boundless. Sara's song reached deep into hearts everywhere.

Thank you for singing your song of joy so brightly and beautifully into my life. Thank you for singing it, even as it is mixed with illness and pain. You are a gift inspiring me to choose joy and encouraging me to welcome joy as an attitude by trusting God with my limitations. Thank you, Sara, for loving us so well.

—*Bonnie Gray*

Though Sara was confined to her home due to her illness, her spirit was NEVER confined there. A disease like this can cause you to look inward, feel sorry for yourself, lose hope, and shut down. But not Sara. Sara has always been present and alive, and she made my life better. More joyful. She has taught me a lot *about* joy. About CHOOSING joy.

In tears, I say this. I know Sara's body has had all it can take. She's ready to leave this life of pain and be with Jesus. She's ready to take a full breath in again. She's ready to go Home and laugh without pain. To run without needing to stop. To have no more restrictions. And it's time. But I'm not ready for Jesus to take her Home. I'm just being honest. I feel heartbroken. And selfish. And I know if she knew, she would tell me to stop crying. Because she's ready to go Home.

Thank you, Sara, for the imprint you've made on my heart. You will live forever on earth through our hearts. So many love you because you have loved so many.

—*Jenni Clayville*

Thank you, Sara, that even through your pain, you stretched up your arms as high as they would reach, to pull down the corners of heaven and share with us your experience of living into the Father's Kingdom. I would not know what the fullness of joy means were it not for you. I would not understand how to live out my strength in the joy of the Lord if I didn't have your example to follow.

You might have lived challenged by location, but your Spirit, your heart, and your person have traveled a wide and long path that is sure to carry on long after you have passed through that thin veil to God's arms.

—*Jenny Rain*

Here was a kindhearted, compassionate woman who was enduring more than most do in their lifetimes. One of the things that stands out to me most about Sara is the amount of grace she has. While her disease reigns over her life she doesn't allow it to rule it. What I mean is she doesn't play the victim. She's open with her readers about her daily life and the struggles she endures but she doesn't point a wagging finger at God and blame Him.

She trusts Him.

I'm not saying she's never questioned God, because even the best of us would. But she lives like the Apostle Paul. She trusts that God can heal her but for His greater purpose has allowed her this "thorn in the side." And if that reason is only to show some people across the globe the grace that she can have and the endurance that He gives her, then His purpose is being fulfilled.

One day Gitzy will be healed and will be whole. She will be able to walk, run, and dance free of the pain that has taken up residence in her body; and I guarantee you she will not dance alone. Her family and friends and readers who live across the world will dance with her.

Over the months that I've daily read her blog I've grown to love her. God has made her dear in my heart.

—*Prudence Landis*

Sara is a beautiful, brave, gifted woman who has lived her faith so loud, lively, and filled with light, you'd never know she can't leave her home. Still, she used her humble, faithful voice, life-giving words, and remarkable spirit to go out into the world and preach the good news, invest in others, pray, encourage, and offer insight.

Truth is, I never met her face-to-face. But she met me right where I was a thousand times, breaking into my heart with her vulnerability, humor, and beauty. She let grace fall all over—in a comment, an e-mail, a handwritten card.

Her reflections told me daily to choose joy, and I certainly can use that reminder every moment, as life blurs past me.

It is a bold choice to see the glorious in the everyday, to live with gratitude wherever God takes you—or doesn't. Sara didn't complain about her condition or not being able to leave her condo. But she didn't gloss over it either—she CHOSE joy, by sharing her story and Who wrote it. She stayed focused on being used by the One Who calls her Home now.

I wasn't prepared, but Sara is. Soon she'll be able to breathe deep, run to her Father in Heaven and to her dad she misses so, and give hugs she's only dreamed of.

I will smile and sing and choose joy in her honor.

—*Mela Kamin*

It felt like we were kindred spirits in so many regards. Above all else my bond with her was based on pure and unconditional love, like I've rarely experienced. She mentored me so, and it was I for the longest time who thought she needed me. *Oh, how I've learned.*

Quite honestly, looking back, I think God placed her in my life to prepare me for my own journey through a life-threatening illness. And to show me what pure love feels like.

—*Vicky Westra*

Sara chose joy every day of her life no matter how much her condition deteriorated. She was a light to me and to so many other people.

Sara is one of the most beautiful, amazing people I have ever known, inside and out. She has been homebound for years and has had to make huge sacrifices, but she never complains. She always smiles. She always loves. She is the best example of Christianity I've ever seen.

I am so, so lucky and blessed to call her a friend. I can't imagine the world without her. I don't want to imagine a world without her. She, however, is happy. I know this without a doubt. She will be running to those gates, not walking. She'll be whole and healed and happy. And I'll be happy for her. But I'll always miss her. Her laugh, her jokes, her obsession with jeans.

—*Ellyn McCall*

۶ — ۶ — ۶

If I had to make a word cloud or a pie chart of the things people mentioned most often when talking about Sara, her laugh would take up a lot of space. And though everyone who knew her mentioned her faith and hope and joy and purpose, those who knew her best also remembered her sarcasm, her teasing, her sharp wit. Sara was no two-dimensional angel; she was a complex woman full of life and love and laughter. She chose joy, she created joy, she shared joy. That's the Gitz we knew.

۶ — ۶ — ۶

People keep writing really beautiful posts about Sara. And make no mistake—they are right about her beauty. And the fact that she couldn't leave her house but made the best of every situation, praised God for it, even. There is nobody like Sara. Never, ever doubt that.

That's who she is. She's the girl who prays for you even though you're the one who should be praying for her. I wasn't impressed by her attitude and her beauty because I read about it on her blog; I was impressed by her attitude and beauty because I saw her live it as we walked each other through some of our hardest days over the last three years. I don't really want to talk about that, though. That's just ours. But rest assured, she is exactly who she represents herself to be on her blog.

So, anyway, don't think for a second that she was ever angelically stoic at all times. Don't think that she was too sick to laugh. Don't think that she didn't have an amazing sense of humor. I don't know of any time I ever laughed harder than when I was talking on the phone, video chatting, e-mailing, tweeting, or texting with her.

She's the kind of friend who, when you send an e-mail to vent about the many, many people in your house, who are all over fifty years old, and therefore have the TV super-loud...

...but accidentally INCLUDE YOUR MOTHER-IN-LAW IN THE E-MAIL, WHO IS SITTING ACROSS THE ROOM FROM YOU...

...will, after having "shouted" an expletive on your behalf and then done nice things to help smooth things over with your (VERY UNDERSTANDING) mother-in-law...

...laugh at you relentlessly and unapologetically with the rest of your friends.

The Gitz I know is snarky. In a loving way.

The Gitz I know will watch an entire movie with you on Skype, eight hundred miles away, making fun of you for how silly you look lying in bed.

The Gitz I know makes up nicknames for those she loves.

The Gitz I know loves food as much as I do. Even if she can't eat a lot of her favorite things because of her allergies.

The Gitz I know is super-creative and loves pretty things, especially if you made them for her.

And the Gitz I know is going to run so fast toward her dad when she finally gets to Heaven that she'll probably knock him right over.

And then she'll laugh so hard that she'll snort (oh yes, she will), which will make her laugh even harder. And unlike here, her lungs will allow her to do that and there will be no sharp pains coursing through her body causing her to cry out in pain during that laugh.

And if letting her go here is what needs to happen for her to laugh without pain? That's worth saying goodbye to the Gitz I know.

—Mandy Hornbuckle